SKYROS

Sunshine for the Soul

Skyros described as 'One of the World's Best Holidays' by *The Sunday Times*, and 'the first and still the best' alternative holiday by *The Guardian*, offers the independent traveller the holiday that opens the heart, expands the mind, recharges the body and uplifts the spirit... sunshine for the soul.

Skyros was Europe's first ever course-based holiday and it remains the world leader in its field. The holidays attract mostly solo holidaymakers from all over the world. A huge majority – over 80 percent – report that the holiday experience had a lasting positive effect on their lives.

In celebration of 40 years since its inception in 1979, co-founders psychologist Dina Glouberman and historian and journalist Yannis Andricopoulos recall their own personal journeys that led to the creation of Skyros and paint, in vivid colours, the development of Skyros through the decades and the contributions of so many.

All parts © Holistic Island Breaks Ltd (2018)

All rights reserved. No part of this
publication may be reproduced without
prior permission from the publishers.

Published by Skyros Books
9 Eastcliff Road,
Shanklin, Isle of Wight PO37 6AA,
United Kingdom
www.skyros.com

Printed by Biddles Books Ltd
Castle House, East Wing Road,
Blackborough End, King's Lynn
Norfolk PE32 1SF
www.biddles.co.uk

ISBN: 978-0-9555456-6-5

With appreciation for all those
who supplied their photographs.

4

Happy
40th
Anniversary

What People Say about Skyros

"I feel blessed to have had the opportunity to stay at such a magical, inspiring and nurturing place."

Richard, Atsitsa, August 2010

"Skyros creates a golden circle in your life. You can wear it as a crown or a bracelet. Either way, your heart knows it must share the change with others."

Alison, The Skyros Centre, June 2011

"This wonderful week at Atsitsa will stay with me forever and will keep me warm on the inside throughout the cold winter in Sweden."

Lena, Atsitsa, September 2016

"Atsitsa was everything I'd hoped it would be - great food, people and courses. Throughly recommend!"

Tania, Atsitsa, October 2014

"I came here exhausted and depleted. A 2 week stay at Atsitsa Bay has restored me so I am floating home. The crystal sea and deep blue sky, vivid memories imprinted of new friends and a renewed love of community and sharing. A fantastic return visit."

J.H, Atsitsa, September 2017

"A truly outstanding and life-changing experience."

Brian, The Skyros Centre, August 2012

"What can I say? The best holidays ever! Thank you Skyros Holidays, for all you have done for me over the years. I'm so glad you exist. With love to you all."

G.M., The Skyros Centre, September 2017

"Atsitsa is the best holiday I've ever been on - now on my third! Each time is different and I have made many new friends."

Penny, Atsitsa, October 2014

"My two weeks in Atsitsa Bay were sensational. I have never experienced such a wonderful nurturing environment and community. It was great fun also and a great place for a solo traveller. A little bit of paradise."

Siobhan, Atsitsa, September 2010

"The courses were very inspirational and enjoyable; thought provoking and energising. Excellent facilitators and trainers."

D.J., The Skyros Centre, September 2017

"The courses exceeded all my expectations, even the comedy sessions that I hadn't planned! The facilitators were so inspiring, I discovered skills I never knew I had."

L.A ., Atsitsa, September 2017

"Met Rose in Atsitsa 2004, we got married 2008. We have just had a Christmas day baby!! George will be told how wonderful Atsitsa is!!"

Graham, Atsitsa, January 2012

"I have felt more genuine friendships in the last week than I've experienced in the previous ten years."

Michael, The Skyros Centre, August 2012

"Wonderful people, and an amazing place."

Marion, The Skyros Centre, August 2017

"I've been coming for 18 years and it keeps getting better!"

Dawne, Atsitsa, August 2011

6

"All that I could have asked for and more! Friendship, good food, great classes, sun, swimming and loads of fun. Thank you!"

Cheryl, Atsitsa, October 2014

"I'm so impressed with the breadth and depth of the courses. I have learnt so much in a relatively short time while having a wonderful time! Overall I've never been to a centre which has this calibre of offerings. The community building process is the best I've experienced! Thank You!"

C.G ., Atsitsa September 2017

"I enjoyed the holiday very much - lovely combination of food for body and soul."

Eamonn, The Skyros Centre, August 2011

"Wow what an experience. Hut life is basic but brilliant. So many memories, so many giggles. Night swimming, star gazing is an absolute must. Give your soul a treat and visit Atsitsa."

Terri, Atsitsa, October 2014

"I have never experienced anything like it before. Bravo!"

L.A ., Atsitsa, September 2017

"This experience met and exceeded all my expectations. I could not be more pleased that I came and I am leaving with a sense of calm and excitement at the positive changes I will be making when I return home."

Danica, The Skyros Centre, August 2012

"I was really impressed by the quality, dedication and humanity of ALL the facilitators. They worked together well and worked with us well."

J.H., Atsitsa, September 2017

"I had a great holiday. My first experience of this and I will definitely do again. Atsitsa Bay is an amazing place, with a beautiful sea cove but made really special by the people there. I did things I haven't done for years and I have made some special friends. Thank you."

Matt, Atsitsa, October 2012

"This is my 10th year in succession and, once again, I feel connected and nourished."

T.A ., Atsitsa, August 2017

"It is indescribable. You have to live it to believe that it is as magic as it is. If everyone had holidays like these the world would be a better place."

Anon, Atsitsa, August 2012

7

"The trip I took to Greece with Skyros Holidays was one of the best in my life. I am 25 years old and traveled all the way from Minnesota, USA. I came by myself but was welcomed and made comfortable by all the staff. Each staff member (including chefs, course teachers, bar assistants and cleaning help, etc) were friendly, fun and professional. The food was fresh and the chefs accommodated to all different diets. The courses were inspiring and enlightening, as well as fun and entertaining. My overall trip and experience was amazing and I came back home a much better person."

Frances, Atsitsa, September 2012

"A magical holiday you need to experience in order to understand how magical it is."

Rana, The Skyros Centre, August 2012

"This was my first experience with this type of community and I loved it!"

J.H., Atsitsa, September 2017

"I finally found all the keys to the locked doors."

Marian, Atsitsa, May 2011

"It's a really inspirational place with a warm heart, a caring philosophy and playfulness. Thank you!"

Sue, Atsitsa, September 2017

"An absolutely incredible experience, all round. I met some amazing people, did great courses and experienced a great deal of emotions!"

Davy, Atsitsa, August 2012

"My sixth visit and it has been amazing! Every experience is unique and has been very special in my life!"

Pam, The Skyros Centre, August 2012

"I had the childhood in Atsitsa that I was denied first time round. I found love, praise, encouragement, nurture and genuine affection and acceptance for the whole of who I am, not what I am. I regard myself as very lucky to have found this place. It is paradise."

Anon, Atsitsa, October 2008

"The community is friendly, open, caring and fun. I want to bottle it so I can take it home and breathe it every day!"

C.S., Atsitsa, August 2017

"Nothing compares - completely mind expanding and heart holding. I would have no hesitation in willing like minds to come and go."

Peter, Atsitsa, September 2011

8

"The Atsitsa staff went out of their way to make us all feel so welcome; accommodated all our wishes and desires. The dancing nights were a real treat. The community was made from the loveliest people; very supportive, interesting and fun. I loved every minute and I leave with such beautiful memories of laughter, love and happiness."

A.H., Atsitsa, August 2017

"This place grows on you day after day and I am sure will pull me back. I will definitely return and bring more people with me. I leave this place as a better person than I was when I came here."

Pusa, Atsitsa, September 2011

"Inspirational, I felt accepted for who I am. The community is friendly, caring and supportive. Very accepting of everyone."

Hazel, Atsitsa, August 2017

"I really, really enjoyed this holiday. Our family did different courses and got together for meals. We had something new to talk about every meal. Parents – bring your teenagers! They'll love it. It was the best and the most relaxing holiday I (we've) had in years."

J.MC., Atsitsa, August 2017

"Met in Atsitsa September 2004. Married in Cheltenham June 2008. What a holiday!"

Amanda & Jim, Atsitsa, July 2008

"You have created a magical kingdom at Atsitsa to celebrate love, life and happiness. Thank you all for a fabulous holiday and for all that you have done to make it so."

Sarah, Atsitsa, September 2008

"I arrived blissfully naive and left blissfully content."

J.Z., Atsitsa, July 2017

"I keep returning to Atsitsa as I haven't found such a fun holiday anywhere else."

Ella, Atsitsa, September 2011

"Whatever your expectations - Skyros Atsitsa will surpass them all...you'll leave glowing...with good health of the body, soul and mind!! yeah!!! I am so glad I came and would ALWAYS recommend staying in a hut too!"

Bo, Atsitsa, August 2010

"Atsitsa opens your heart and helps you deal with what happens next ....."

Pauline, Atsitsa, September 2011

9

"The accommodation was so much better than I was expecting! I thought a hut would encompass a cross between camping and festival but they are simple, lovely, clean, peaceful and most importantly cool at night."

J.M., Atsitsa, August 2017

"Forget the 'alternative' or 'new age' labels - it is a great holiday."

Peter, Atsitsa, September 2011

"After my first life changing visit 15 years ago, returning to Skyros has confirmed that the magical emotional safety net is still very much in place."

Caroline, Atsitsa, September 2011

"It's a different experience each year. This is my 4th visit consecutively and I'll be back next year for another amazing experience."

P.S., Atsitsa, August 2017

"I can't find the words to express how I feel. Can't wait to come back!!"

Nickie, Atsitsa, September 2011

"I love it here, my third year running and I will be back. This is a very special place and community and I am so grateful to have it in my life."

H.T., Atsitsa, July 2017

"So much more than a holiday, Atsitsa is a life-changing experience and I will be back."

Caroline, Atsitsa, September 2011

"The food is the best I have ever had in my life! Amazing! Being a vegetarian with coeliac disease means food is rarely a pleasure on holiday."

H.G., Atsitsa, July 2017

"It's like a garden of Eden peopled by friends who want to bring out the best in each other and help each other to know themselves as unique and special."

Catherine, Atsitsa, August 2011

"An instant community with whom one feels as close and relaxed as with great friends. All in a hypnotically beautiful setting."

Anon, Atsitsa, August 2012

"Atsitsa is the closest place to heaven on earth I have ever been to. The beauty of nature and the heartful connections make a holiday there a transformational experience. Pure magic!"

Malcolm, Atsitsa, February 2011

10

"Atsitsa is my second home. It is always a joy to be in this wonderful, magical place with such open-minded, honest and truly inspiring people."

Rachel, Atsitsa, August 2011

"The group energy and trust can equip you with the courage to reveal things closest to your heart that would never happen elsewhere - such a liberation."

Jamie, Atsitsa, August 2011

"Really, this is a place where family is formed. A new family, not a traditional one, but a family none-the-less. My heart leaves full of love and life."

B.H., The Skyros Centre, August 2017

"We arrived with rounded shoulders from carrying the burden of a very difficult year. We left with our shoulders back, head held high, re-energized and ready to enter the battle ground again. Atsitsa worked its magic!"

Karen, Atsitsa, August 2012

"This was my eighth visit to the Grange and if anything it was even better than before! Needless to say I'll be back again!"

Penny, The Grange, April 2017

"I read many reviews before travelling and thought it too good to be true - I was proved wrong. Amazing experience."

Colette, Atsitsa, July 2010

"I don't know another place I can meet such great people in such a beautiful, unspoiled environment and so quickly have a sense of belonging - not to mention the fantastic courses on offer with top people."

Sarah, Atsitsa, August 2011

"Our group continue to be in close contact now we're (reluctantly!) back in the UK, so the fortnight's experience will last and last."

Marion, The Skyros Centre, June 2008

"The best in the world at what they do. Truly unforgettable."

Sue I., The Skyros Centre, August 2017

"An inspiring holiday which unlocks doors but also exudes such warmth."

Rosie, Atsitsa, August 2011

"A wonderful, magical place... I will be back!"

Fiona, Atsitsa, June 2010

"A real holiday for the soul."

Alan, Atsitsa, June 2010

11

Yannis and Dina, 1977, in the backyard of what was to become The Skyros Centre

Table of Contents

Introduction

It is my absolute pleasure to introduce this book celebrating 40 years of Skyros holidays. The continuance of these life-changing retreats and holidays and the outstanding ethos that underpins them has become an all-consuming passion for me over the past ten years. It is a privilege to co-direct alongside inspirational Skyros founders Dina Glouberman and Yannis Andricopoulos.

My own involvement began in 1990 with a much-anticipated holiday to Atsitsa, one of the two Skyros holiday centres in Greece. I'd seen the flyer in *Health & Fitness* magazine a year or two before and I'd pored through the brochure, deciding on my holistic courses. I loved the idea of 'areté' and I'd always been entranced by the fact that we function at so little of our true capacity as human beings. At that time, I was particularly interested in complementary medicine and wanted to learn more.

And so the adventure began. I loved it so much that I returned to Atsitsa for three months at a time for the following three summers as a 'work scholar', helping out in return for the opportunity to take courses. I was ecstatic pretty much the entire time. I would do my very best, working hard, mopping the floors and making beds. In the evenings we would all meet at Maria's taverna or go into the village, often returning with the vegetable cart in the morning. I made some amazing friends and many I'm still in touch with now.

The thing I most loved about living in Atsitsa, in particular, was the open-minded, fun-loving and supportive community. We all looked out for each other through all the ups and downs with everyone working towards fulfilling their dreams in life. The whole atmosphere was one of generosity and respect for one another and our potentials.

Returning to London, Yannis and I became colleagues, firm friends and partners. We've lived and worked together harmoniously and creatively ever since. In 2004 we moved from London to the Isle of Wight, setting up The Grange as an offshoot of Skyros. Later, in 2007, Skyros relocated its HQ from London to The Grange. We both love Skyros and have given it our total care and attention.

If you're reading this book, you may well have been on a Skyros holiday once or many times and will know the magic of Skyros for yourself. You have become part of the ever-expanding Skyros community including extraordinary, talented and warm-hearted facilitators and staff. As you know, should you bump into someone connected with Skyros, you have an instant and unspoken connection. Skyros is like a huge family.

If you've yet to go, then know that you'll be warmly received whether your intention is to holiday on your own for the first time, develop a skill or try something challenging and new. Or perhaps, like me, you want to take a good look at your life and consider the alternatives in front of you.

We hope that you will enjoy these stories and photographs as much as we do as we mark 40 years of Skyros, retracing its early, pioneering beginnings and subsequent development into the trailblazing, vibrant community based holiday that has touched the hearts and minds of thousands of people through the decades.

Read on for more from Dina and Yannis whose honest and personal accounts describe how it is possible to follow a vision and make a small but significant contribution to our culture.

Christine Schulz
Managing Director
e: christine@skyros.com

1. Skyros Island, Greece
Home to Skyros Holidays

Atsitsa's main building in a bay where nature feels at home

Atsitsa Bay, one of the Earth's true beauty spots

18

The medieval St George's Church under the village castle

Skyros village from the fishermen's harbour

19

The castle that was originally built in the second millennium BC

Palamari, a prehistoric town linked commercially even to the Middle East

When a rock turns into a church

Skyros' beautiful countryside where Nature can breathe once again

A clever man. He knows how to avoid the rush hour

22

Atsitsa's sensational sunset

The village's sandy beach from the hill above

23

Dina Glouberman at The Skyros Centre in the early years

2. Creating a world that heals

A personal history of founding a symbolic community on the Greek Island of Skyros*

by Dr. Dina Glouberman

Summer, 1977, and Yannis and I and six-month-old Ari spend the summer camped in the garden of a house on the Greek island of Skyros. Two summers later, this house is to become the home of the Skyros Centre, our first holiday community on Skyros Island.

Creating Skyros Holidays was and is one of the miracles of my life. How often do you get the chance to create a mini-world with values you believe in, and on a Greek island?

Like so many creative endeavours, it was born out of a meeting between dreaming and despairing. At that moment, we were confronting the failure of the dreams of the sixties to materialise in the way we expected. When we despair of the world we live in, yet carry a picture of how it might be and a faith that it is possible to go there, the moment is always charged with creative power.

Recently, as I have worked with the growing phenomena of burnout, I have begun to understand why modern society spawns both burnout and places like Skyros as two sides of the same coin. We live in a world where our choices go far beyond those of our parents. We are not expected to have the one career or even relationship for life, nor do we wish to stop growing and developing when we reach middle age. Yet we constantly come up against contradictions in the world and in ourselves that keep us stuck and hurting.

Against this background, we burn out when we come to an end of a particular road and cannot acknowledge it because of some central picture of ourselves we want to preserve. Our soul is whispering and we are not

---

* This article is adapted from Dina Glouberman's new memoir: Glouberman, Dina, *Into the Woods and Out Again: A memoir of love, madness and transformation* (London: Sphinx, 2018)

25

listening. Skyros, and places like it, offer an opportunity to people to step back and listen to their soul in order to let go of past identities and find a new way of living. It gives choice a chance.

This was also our own precious chance to make a new choice.

We need to backtrack a bit to the previous winter, when Yannis and I spent a weekend at my friend Bridget's home. Bridget and I were struggling with the powers that be at Kingston Polytechnic, where we were both Senior Lecturers, and dreaming of another way.

That weekend the idea of creating a centre in Greece emerged. Why not do something in Greece? Yannis could organise the Greek side, I could run groups, and Bridget could run sociology seminars on related topics. It was a wonderful idea, but Bridget dropped out soon after, and I doubt that, left to my own devices, I would have actually carried out the plan. It was Yannis that made sure it became a reality.

Yannis was suffering from the seventies. The academic world, so lush in the sixties, had dried up. Lecturing jobs were like gold dust. As I read somewhere, a PhD in History was not so much a stepping-stone as a millstone.

He was working as the London Correspondent for a Greek paper, but the pay was derisory. He did some sums and figured out that running a centre might be a viable way to earn a living. No sooner seen than done. Within days he was out in Greece looking for a place.

I remember reading that the Findhorn Foundation community in Scotland would not have been founded if co-founder Peter Caddy had not been unemployed at the time. If Yannis had gotten one of the lecturing jobs he applied for, or if I had liked the one I had, there would have been no Skyros Centre.

As I was falling asleep the night after he left for Greece, I had a kind of waking dream. I was walking on a beach and a wise man came walking toward me. He took my hand and let me know without words that there was hope, and dreams could come true.

Yannis went straight to the Sporades Islands, a constellation of islands north-east of Athens, popular with the Greeks but little known abroad at that time. It includes Skiathos – the most touristic of this island group even then, and more recently the location for the film *Mama Mia* – as well as Alonissos, Skopelos, and Skyros.

He came to Skyros last and there he found a large derelict house that had been a school. The minute he saw it, he said to himself, "This is it."

26

He phoned me and we agreed to buy it. The Skyros adventure was about to begin for real.

This project could only have come out of that unlikely partnership between, on the one hand, an American Jewish psychologist with a background in Socialist Zionist communal summer camps (at a time when Socialist Zionist was not an oxymoron) and in humanistic psychotherapy and personal development workshops, and on the other, a left-wing Greek whose career trajectory in journalism and politics had been messed up by the Greek dictatorship just when he was beginning to make a name for himself.

I had the ability to create the kind of social, psychological and spiritual world that is a hothouse for transformation, plus a personal yearning for community, connectedness, meaning, and consciousness change. Yannis was able to create the bricks and mortar physical world to house this symbolic venture, and also had a tremendous drive to begin and to expand at moments when I might well have given up.

What we shared was our quirky individualistic creativity, and an underlying set of values to do with social justice, plus a basic ability to do the sums. Less favourably, we shared a serious lack of experience at business management, a weakness that became more significant as participants stopped being tolerant of our foibles and began to have more conventional expectations.

Years later, I read an article in which a business angel talked of what she needed to see in a business to make her feel it was a good bet for investing. She looked for the presence of one visionary, and one accountant type to run the show. We were two visionaries and no accountant type.

But it worked, beyond our wildest dreams. My original picture as I described it to myself was of "twelve people to a Greek island," and I expected it to go on for three or four years. Now, almost forty years later, more than 30,000 people have passed through our doors. Increasingly they have included conventionally successful mainstream professionals rather than the eccentric alternative types we tended to attract in the early pioneering years, and a large majority of them have made profound life changes as a result of their stay in Skyros.

My view now is that our souls brought the two of us to Skyros and sensed what was to come, while we, in the sense of our everyday personalities, had very little idea what we were about to set into motion.

At that time, the world of New Age therapies, complementary medicine, and the notion of mind, body and spirit had not yet become big business. Nor did special interest holidays of any kind have a significant presence in the

27

tourism world, with the exception of Club Med, founded in 1950. What we were doing turned out to be not just an idealistic professional venture but a new kind of tourism.

We were pioneers at the forefront of a sea change in holidays.

Journalists from all over the world came to see for themselves what the fuss was about. Full-page spreads appeared in all the major papers and magazines. The journalists often came to mock, and then stayed to praise us. Almost consistently, the articles were paeons to this life-changing, laughter filled, joyous experience.

The usual story, especially if the reporter was British, would be that they were at first incredibly cynical but eventually they themselves had a wonderful life-changing experience and had made friends for life. The British were so allergic to anything to do with the inner life or alternative living at that time that even sympathetic journalists felt they wouldn't be believed unless it was clear they were not hippy dippy themselves.

As we became known and successful, and as it became clear more generally that people were bored with beach holidays, the special interest and all-inclusive activity holidays burgeoned. A number of smaller centres featuring one or another of the alternative approaches began to appear. These were quite often started by people who had worked or had been participants in Skyros, and who shared many of our ideas. I don't think any had the wonderful range of holistic activities combined with an intentional community atmosphere that made Skyros so unique.

The Guardian called us 'the first and still the best'. [1]

There is also something else that I cannot account for by simply describing what we did. People laughed, danced and played, as well as sinking into a deeper part of themselves than they thought possible. Miracles were commonplace. Relationships were formed in a kind of crucible so that people felt they had known one another forever, and often became friends for life. As one participant told me, if you met anyone anywhere in the world and they said they had been in Skyros, you immediately knew you could have a deep connection with them.

Many felt this was the turning point in their lives or that it was their best holiday ever - or both. Everywhere I went in the world I'd meet someone who'd been to Skyros and had a wonderful story to tell about their transformation there.

I believe that this something else emerges when we intend to create

28

something from the soul, and are willing not only to foster love and truth, but to work towards our own transformation. My old friend, the late Max Furlaud, used to say, 'In Skyros, every Thursday night at the end of a two week session, the angels gather round.' This is a kind of grace, the gift of the soul.

Looking back, I am struck by the way that I, a young woman from Brooklyn already living in a country that was not my own, could go to a relatively remote village in Greece to make it the home of a spiritual venture. Yet I never had any doubts.

Perhaps it is because it represented on some level the coming together of the worlds I had inherited from my mother and father. My mother was a Mediterranean woman imbued with the pioneering spirit of the early days of Palestine and Israel. My father was a spiritual and psychological seeker, as well as a natural educator, and was particularly taken by the whole new world of humanistic psychology.

Put them together, mix in this unique partnership between myself and Yannis, and voilá, Skyros Holidays.

I. The Skyros Centre: Our First Summer

Summer, 1979. Yannis and I are walking down the cobblestone path of Skyros village carrying luggage and two babies. Ari is two years old and Chloe, three months. We are expecting fifteen people to come in three days for our first group. Yannis' father, Mitso, will also be joining us from Athens. The session, including accommodation, two meals, groups, and other activities, costs £45 per person if you share a large room at the centre, and £55 if you stay in village rooms. Almost all have opted to stay in the house.

We turn a corner and catch a glimpse of the centre-to-be. It has no doors or windows, and it is only half a house. The rest is a building site.

We managed to make sure that the doors and windows were on by the time the people came. The rest of the house was not finished. And this is where we would sleep, run groups, eat, and generally have a life. So we started our first session with all of us living in half a house with a "kitchen" that was basically four unplastered concrete walls and no roof, equipped with a two-ring gas hob and a supply of water. It eventually took the builder only a few days to finish the house, but of course he didn't get round to it till after the season was over.

In case you ever need to know, *avrio* is the Greek word for *manana*.

Yannis, the two babies, Mitso and I all slept in a tiny room that had just enough floor space for our mattresses. We had put a partition in the big room so that we could have this extra little bedroom. Another somewhat larger room housed the men. The largest room, which ours opened into, was for the women. As always, an inner adventure attracted more women than men.

We all shared one bathroom with two doors, one door opening from the men's room and the other from the women's room – and none from our room.

The nights were hellish. I'd wake in the night because Chloe needed to be fed and changed, but I had to fumble around in complete darkness because if I turned on the light, I might wake Ari, who might cry and wake everyone else up.

Mornings weren't too good either. I'd walk into the bathroom and then someone would call me, and I'd walk out, toothbrush in one hand, baby in the other hand. The door would then shut and lock behind me because someone had gone in the other door.

Little Chloe, bless her heart, became an absolutely serene angel the moment we hit Athens. Something in her settled down in Greece. All summer she only cried when she was hungry. And Ari was just old enough to enjoy the attentions of so many amazing people. We certainly didn't have a lot of "quality time" with the kids that summer.

I have said that there was no real kitchen, but also there was no real cook. We took the idea of community seriously and thought the participants would just muck in and make it all happen.

The staff, besides Yannis and me, included one other group leader. In the first session, it was my friend and colleague Silke Ziehl, who offered a bodywork group, and went on to lead groups in Skyros almost every year thereafter, and in the second, it was Jacques Salzer from Paris, who offered a theatre and mime course.

We were also blessed with the help of a wonderful young artist named Joe Olubo who had offered his services as a gardener after seeing our little *Time Out* advert for participants. Unbelievably, we didn't actually think we needed a staff. Yannis had shrugged and said, "Come along. But there won't be much to do." This became a standing joke.

Joe was a tall, black, handsome guy with a relaxed and warm temperament, a wonderful sense of humour, and, luckily for us, a willingness and ability to do just about everything. He shopped, cooked, got the participants cooking,

30

gardened, took people on walks, and generally worked non-stop to make the whole thing possible. Without him, I don't know how we would have survived.

I recently learned that Joe died in 1990, aged only thirty-eight. Blessings to you Joe, wherever you are. We loved you so much.

Truly, we had no idea what running the Skyros Centre would entail. There's an old Jewish story about how God went around to various tribes asking them if they wanted the Ten Commandments. As each tribe checked it out, finding perhaps that they weren't allowed to kill, or to steal, or to commit adultery, they turned it down one by one. But the Jews simply said *Na'aseh V'nishma*, which literally means, We will do and we will listen. In other words, we agree to do it before we know what it involves.

Na'aseh V'nishma must have been engraved on our hearts.

Would we have done it if we'd known? After all, I had a full-time job, with two small children, clients and therapy groups. Every corner of my life was spoken for even before we started Skyros, and I only rested in order to get energy to do more work.

But it never occurred to us to consider the downside of anything we thought was worth doing. This is what I later called "soul esteem", the willingness to follow the inner voice wherever it takes you, however unworthy you feel, and at almost any price.

I had no self-esteem to speak of at the time, but I did have soul esteem.

To put it another way, whoever was directing our movie had no trouble making us an offer we couldn't refuse.

The truth is that no matter how hard it got, I loved it. It was as if we'd invited people to a party on a Greek island and they all came. Most were from my Open Circle Group in London. A few came from our adverts in Time Out. There was a whole contingent of French participants whom Jacques brought with him, many of whom could hardly speak English. All were prepared to be pioneers, so despite the problems, it was a great party.

On the first day of the first session, Jacqueline and Maryse, two of the women from Jacque's group, arrived early, and Maryse told me she spoke almost no English. "So you will do Silke's bodywork group?" I asked. No, she'd come for my group.

We had a Belgian participant who spoke French and English fluently and he heroically translated for us during the whole group. When Maryse took centre stage in the groupwork, all the work was conducted with a two-way translation. I'm not sure how much I understood but it seemed to work. I still remember one piece of psychodrama ending with her shouting "Maryse vit."

Yannis was meanwhile working nonstop, including liaising with the Greeks, finding rooms for participants, and generally making sure that the whole thing worked, and when it didn't, making sure that something was done about it. And I somehow, as if by magic, knew how to create a space where people could feel at home in themselves and with each other, often for the first time in their lives. I think I had an instinct for creating the kind of communication structures and attitudes that would encourage safety, exploration, support and truth.

Perhaps it was my soul that knew how to do it, while I was a neurotic young thing. Indeed, maybe my soul knew what that neurotic young thing, and so many others like me, needed and longed for. Certainly now, almost forty years later, the structure and atmosphere are still held as if by the walls of the place, even though all the staff and participants are changed, and I myself am not there most of the time.

The intention always was to create a world that heals. This did not simply mean a healing of individual past hurts, but rather something more ambitious: an attempt to create a healthy culture. This culture must be one that encourages us to come home to ourselves, to honour our true selves relative to others, and to commit ourselves to the most universal values we can find. Such a world cannot help but heal us into new ways of living, loving and contributing.

On a personal level, we saw Skyros as a hothouse for personal transformation. On a social level, it was about creating a different kind of society in which people could live together with respect and love. As time went on, we evolved the spiritual level, the sense that Skyros is one of many centres of light around the world that contribute to the spiritual fabric of the world.

It was, indeed, years before I used the word "spiritual" explicitly because I was so allergic to the organised religion of my childhood. A wonderful free-spirited nun convinced me that this level needed to be named.

Holidays are a perfect way to accomplish these ambitious intentions because when you temporarily leave behind your everyday life, including the people and responsibilities of that life, you can look afresh at everything safely and without commitment. Moreover, you can do it in a beautiful, warm place with beautiful, warm people. As you feel the benefits of it all, the ties to your old patterns loosen naturally, and you become open to something new.

I knew instinctively, both from my experiences and my own deep yearnings, that the alchemy of community, personal development courses,

Greek island holiday, and seekers coming together from all over the world would have the power to transform lives in a matter of days.

The personal development groups seemed to be the centrepiece of the experience, and certainly were in personal development centres around the world. But for me, it was the community that was the real chamber of transformation.

Skyros would not have taken this form had I not myself been longing for a community, Always in my life I had been confronted by the split between community atmospheres in which I flourished, and institutional environments in which I shrank into myself. These began in childhood and adolescence with my conventional Jewish day school and my Socialist Zionist summer camps which were run as communities. I used to think I had two personalities, one in school and one in camp. Then there was my radical Brandeis University undergraduate programme (starring Herbert Marcuse and Abraham Maslow) where I was challenged to explore, followed by a rigid postgraduate Clinical Psychology programme where I was seen as someone who needed social control.

Just before we started Skyros, I was facilitating weekend personal development groups filled with honesty and love and then confronting awful Polytechnic politics on Monday morning. I literally shrank as I walked down the Polytechnic hall. So I knew something about the kind of environment which would make me happy and open to transformation.

I also knew that this was not just true for me. In my picture, institutions are built of walls of brick and stone, indifferent to our coming and going; if we don't like them, we vote with our feet and get out. Communities have walls made of people; if we don't like what is happening, we move ourselves into a better shape by being both responsible and responsive.

Now, there is mounting evidence that people who live in healthy communities where they are known, cared for, valued, and have a role, are generally healthier and live longer. [2] Then, we knew it intuitively because people were obviously so much happier.

But it was not just any old community we needed to form. We cannot go back to traditional communities where we are held warmly, but our souls are not given breathing room. Yes, we are greeted, known, and cared for, but we are also controlled by old rules, roles and expectations and in particular by that great social control mechanism called gossip.

This community had to be one you created and let go of in two weeks, and one where you could be accepted simply and unconditionally for who and what you are, and what you are becoming, and not for what you have been or should be. In a sense, it offers us a transformative new culture, one with human values, and a respect for what is truly important.

I later called this kind of community a "soul community. Only a soul community can free us to become ourselves in a way that allows us to maintain our connectedness to others. I used to go around in the early days of Skyros asking people 'Would you rather be loved or be free?' In a soul community, these are indivisible.

In such an atmosphere everyone, including the staff, is learning and growing, and has a sense of belonging and a commitment to truth. A community in which those who facilitate the process are not honest about themselves is never a true soul community.

Skyros is therefore based on a series of interlocking communication structures, including the community meetings, the staff groups, the *oekos* or home groups, the courses, the work groups, co-listening in pairs, the communication with oneself. These simple and safe communication structures open the possibility of 'real talk' and 'real listening' – speaking and listening in which we are at once fully present to one another and to ourselves.

These structures – and a staff selected not only for their skills but for their qualities of authenticity and warmth – have successfully created soul community session after session for forty years. This consistency is remarkable given a constantly evolving staff team and participants.

To create this community quickly, people were encouraged to let go almost immediately of their normal rules of interaction and communication and invited to tell the truth to someone they hadn't met before yesterday, but might become their lifelong friend. I was used to this fairly immediate open communication in the personal development world, which was full of get-to-know you and let-go-of-your defences kind of exercises, and was an environment in which truth, intimacy, and loving support were always encouraged.

I also knew that people had to participate actively in taking care of this world, just as they would in their own home, so that they weren't passive guests but active members of the community.

It was considered a rather odd idea to have people come on holiday and join work groups. Yet, I always took for granted that this needed to be part of the experience.

This probably was an unconscious reflection of my summer camp experiences in the community oriented Habonim camps, where working in the cornfield was part of our daily schedule. I realised this only years later when a BBC producer intent on making a film about us recognised the similarity with his own childhood experiences of Habonim, and asked about it.

It was also clear to me that building community needed to include giving people a say in their everyday lives. Hence, we held weekly community gatherings as well as a daily breakfast get-together called Demos, which is Greek for 'the people.' Again, it was rather an odd thing to have meetings on a holiday, but they did help create that unique Skyros experience of another type of society.

The normal boundaries between the experiences of staff and participants were softened. Not only would participants have an opportunity to participate in running the place, but staff would have a learning and growth experience no less powerful than that of participants. Moreover, we saw it as our responsibility to contribute financially and culturally to the welfare of the local Greek community. The whole thing had to be an evolving community on all levels.

And the process can't finish when people leave the premises; it needs to be supported and maintained back home. For this, we need bridges. One important bridge is continuing contact with the people with whom we have the kind of deep connection that is forged in a soul community. Such a bank of people holds us at that delicate moment when we are peeping out from the chaos of not-knowing into new ways of being.

How did it work in practice? It was not very different from the way it works today, so many years later.

People would be greeted the first evening or morning with the introductory community gathering, where they would be encouraged to get to know each other, integrate, learn about Skyros, each other, and themselves.

There were also two other community gatherings during the session – in the middle and at the end – where people were encouraged to have a voice, reflect on their experience, say what they liked and didn't like, solve problems together. I made up a rule: *No complaints without suggestions.*

I was so fixed on the idea of community problem solving, that when people tried to say they had no problems and just wanted to dance, I would demand that they find some. How could we solve problems if there weren't any? Eventually this boundless idealism gave way to relief when nothing problematic was raised.

Besides these special community gatherings, each morning after breakfast we had the Demos get-together, where we made announcements, taught Greek, asked for suggestions, gave thoughts for the day, and generally communicated about anything a community member felt was important. A different participant ran this each day.

Then there'd be work group time, which could mean helping with the cooking, cleaning the toilets, sweeping up, setting the table, and so on. Some people actually preferred cleaning the toilets. "I wanted to get into my shit," one put it. It was particularly attractive to loners who were pleased to find a job they could do on their own.

As in most organisations, what tended to transpire was that one participant would jump in and carry most of the work. Because we were into personal development, by the second week our eager beaver had worked out that this was an old role he or she didn't want to be playing any more, and would opt out. The lynch pin of the kitchen would disappear.

While the work groups were going on, the staff would be having a staff meeting, which always included checking in with each other emotionally, as well as talking about what was going on with participants, getting group supervision, and planning the day. This became an important part of the day for the group leaders, who were used to working on their own in their everyday life, and loved being part of a team and learning from each other.

I remember Pulitzer prize winning novelist Alison Lurie telling me that the staff meetings were her reason for coming back to Skyros to teach again and again.

After the staff meetings, the three-hour morning courses began. Afternoons after lunch were for beach going, odd workshops anyone wanted to put on, walks to various beauty spots, talk and more talk, especially around the kitchen table. Evenings were wonderful visits to tavernas around town and by the sea. And then there were the parties and the dancing and the laughter.

If it was your birthday in Skyros, everyone made a wonderful fuss over you all day. I decided that your Skyros age was made up of the first and second number of your chronological age. So if you were 58, you could be 13, or even 4. Even today, people love this concept. Some participants began to time their holidays to coincide with their birthdays.

In the midst of all the community and group work, we needed a communication structure that was one-to-one. We evolved the notion of "co-listening", a safe and powerful structure for talking, or more like thinking out loud, in the presence of another person, that enabled people to recognise and resolve whatever was nagging at them below the surface.

You could see pairs of people all over the centre and village with eyes closed, speaking and listening to each other in a beautiful way. I loved it. It all had the smell of community at its best, against the fabulous background of blue skies, whitewashed little houses, and Greeks who tended to look more ancient than they were.

Later, when I was involved in gatherings of people running growth centres around the world, including Esalen and Omega, I discovered that while other centres might have a community atmosphere for their team of young helpers, there was no attempt to create a community for administrators, teachers and participants. I was often asked how I had come up with something so unique.

When I myself taught in some of these centres, and found that I never had a chance to get together with the other staff in a meaningful way, it left me feeling a bit lonely and disappointed. I appreciated even more the structure that we had created in Skyros that kept everyone connected with each other and with the whole community.

Beyond the roots of these holidays in our own personal histories, there was the importance of the cultural world of the 60's in which we came of age, and the simple fact that we really did believe that we could change the world. Only later did the cynicism set in.

Our little contribution was to create a mini world that had some of the qualities that the world at large was missing and to hope for a ripple effect. We didn't kid ourselves that what we could do in Skyros would be equally easy to do in our everyday lives. It was a short-term holiday experience, with no future commitments weighing it down, and people were not competing for status or jobs or money. They were there to surrender to the warmth of the physical world and the community, enjoy life and learn something new.

However, it did give people the experience of the life enhancing benefits of community, and inspired many to go home and bring something back to their everyday lives.

Poet Hugo Williams called it "a holiday to take home with you." That was exactly what I hoped it would be.

The Skyros Centre worked amazingly in that people did feel at home, and had wonderful times, and life changing experiences. And the staff were as transformed by the experience as the participants, and wanted to come back year after year to be part of it.

In fact, many participants said they didn't dare to go back because the first time was so magical. Thankfully, they often took the risk, and found it different, but equally wonderful.

As the years went by, I'd get more and more letters from people telling me that they now had a new group of friends, a new job, new partner, a new country. Everywhere I went in the world, someone would recognise me and tell me how Skyros had changed their lives, and they were now living where they were, or with whomever they were living, or doing what they were doing because of that turning-point moment. I'd get photos of babies whose parents had met in Skyros, or indeed who had been conceived there, with the caption "another Skyros baby."

Indeed, as people went home and regularly quit their jobs, I got frightened for them, and made a rule that you couldn't quit your job for forty days after coming back from Skyros. But I never met anyone who was sorry they'd taken the risk, or who didn't feel that their new life was worth it. Since people often came to Skyros at a moment in their lives when they yearned for change, Skyros may well have been the catalyst for a long awaited transformation.

But it didn't always work as well for me. It is true that some of my highest and most magical moments happened in Skyros. The memory picture that comes to mind is a simple one of being part of a whole group of participants and staff laughing, talking, and singing around a delicious dinner at a taverna by the sea in Linaria, the port town, knowing at that very moment that this was what I had always wanted and that my life just couldn't be better.

But some of my lowest and most painful moments also happened in Skyros, when I was feeling exhausted, weighed down by the responsibility for so much and so many. The most painful learning for me was that when you create a community experience because you yearn for community, everyone else has it but you.

You are backstage making it happen.

II. The Skyros Centre: Second Summer

The first summer of the Skyros Centre was a crazy attempt to create a wonderful holiday experience in a half-finished overcrowded building site of a house. It worked because the people who came were pioneers. They loved everything, no matter how rough and tough it was, and we all worked together to create those magical times.

By the second summer, we could afford to breathe a sigh of relief.

38

The house was finished, and everything was so much smoother. But by the second summer, people came with expectations – and complaints. We were discovering what theatre people know about the second night of a play.

We were now running four two-week sessions. I would finish teaching at the Polytechnic one day, we would go to Skyros the next, and at the end of the eight weeks, we'd close down the Centre, and I'd start teaching the next day.

We never thought of keeping an office open in the summer months while we were in Skyros. In our minds, the Skyros Centre was simply wherever we were, so if we were on the island, we did not expect to have a presence anywhere else.

Since we rented out our house while we were away, if you phoned us you'd probably get a French or a Spanish voice answering, not knowing what you were talking about. If you hadn't booked by the time we left for the summer, you weren't going to be able to book at all. You either gave up or showed up.

So many people just turned up, despite the fact that it was a real odyssey to get there, that we had no idea how many people were coming for a session. Once, from thinking we had a near empty session, we ended with a whole influx of people who had not managed to book, and of course they were the ones who complained that the Centre was overcrowded. One member of that group orchestrated a little revolution, which rather shocked me, but in the end, it all got absorbed into the happy spirit of the place.

The vast majority of the people who came to Skyros at that time did not really expect the kind of modern conveniences that they do nowadays. But still there were sometimes serious gripes, and looking back, I can certainly see why.

People would arrive at the Centre, having painfully tried to follow our minimal typewritten instructions giving approximate bus and ferry times. They'd taken a city bus from a nightmarish warren of a bus station, and then a public ferry to the island. They may or may not have been lucky enough to meet someone on the way with whom they could travel.

Occasionally they took the wrong ferry, as when Hilary and Kurt took a boat called SS Skyros which was not, however, going to Skyros, and spent three days getting to us. However, in that time they fell in love and eventually married. Sometimes a mistake is not a mistake.

When our participants finally got to the main square of Skyros, they would search desperately for the Centre. Our typewritten direction read

"Follow the main road towards the sea", so they were expecting a tarmacked road, not a cobblestone street, and you could go towards the sea in either direction. If in trouble, we told them to ask for *spiti* Andricopoulos (the house of Andricopoulos) or for one of our neighbours, Nikos or Costas. If they asked for the Skyros Centre instead, they were directed back to the village square, which was after all the centre of Skyros.

Then, when they'd finally get to us, and ask for their room, they might be told, "Yannis is sleeping right now. When he wakes up he will find you a room." And I don't mean "Yannis will take you to your room". I mean that he literally had to find a room we could rent from among our neighbours' houses.

It really was as bad as that, and we didn't even know this wasn't okay. A slick tourist organisation we weren't.

Nor did we or anyone else expect that. It was a time when the perfection of an experience was not considered to depend on the perfection of the facilities.

But when one group created a little skit to show the importance of the moment of welcoming, we realised that that no matter what the practical difficulties were, we needed to open our hearts to our new participants, and make them feel at home from the first minute. It was the spirit of our presence that mattered most.

The rooms people stayed in were very basic. Some did not have indoor bathrooms. Others had uncomfortable old beds, or were filled with the paraphernalia of the landladies, or had no real wardrobes. As one participant said of his tiny outdoor loo, "It is the only place where you can sit on the loo, take a shower, and brush your teeth without moving an inch." At the time, I thought none of this mattered. Surely the magic was worth suffering a bit of inconvenience!

And in a way, this was true. Nowadays, we meet people in Athens, take them on our chartered bus either to the airport for the Athens-Skyros plane, or all the way to the island, escort them to the Centre, give them a welcome drink, and show them to their beautiful modern rooms and apartments. But I'm not sure that people complained much more about those primitive rooms than they do about one or another limitation of the vastly superior accommodation of today. It's all so relative, so dependent on our expectations, so embedded in the context of the whole experience.

In many ways, I was an unreconstructed child of the sixties. I was so into being authentic that I didn't even realise I was allowed to write the speech I gave on the first evening. I thought that if it wasn't organic and spontaneous I was being phony. It was okay to structure lectures at my Polytechnic, but not here. I'd appear on the first evening, and hope for inspiration. If I was nervous enough, I might have a few glasses of wine to inspire the inspiration.

I certainly didn't know that you have to separate the role of therapist from things like the organisation of the kitchen or the collection of money for a coach. And since Yannis was often in London, it turned out that dealing with Greek workmen who spoke no English with my rather pathetic Greek was also part of my brief.

In the first few summers I was the centre of everything from the most mundane to the most spiritual, and organising the "mundane" has never been my strong point. To get me from one room to another without someone stopping me, saying "Dina, Dina", participants sometimes offered to be my 'bodyguards' to enable me to keep moving.

But I wanted to make sure everyone felt welcomed and at home, and thought I was the one to do it because on some level, it was our home we were inviting them to for this wonderful party.

What fascinated me most was the evolution of our notions of community.

The community meetings were central to this evolution because this was where each session worked out its own relationship to their lives at the Centre. What one session's community meetings created, the next destroyed, until eventually we were left with a stable sense of what was important. The structure we have today is based on what we had from the very first day, developed and refined with the important learnings we gained from community meetings and staff meetings.

One community meeting that comes to mind is the time we had seven or eight rather anarchic Greeks as participants and one of them decided that he didn't want to join a work group. It was his holiday after all. He didn't just skive off work, as I'm sure many people did. He brought it to the community meeting to discuss.

The Greeks love their politics.

The question was debated at length. Should he do what he wanted, in the name of individual freedom? Or should he be told that it just wasn't fair, and that if he did this, so would everyone else and then where would we be?

I tried to steer the discussion away from moral undertones and overtones, and eventually the decision was that he should do as he chose.

As it turned out, refusing to work was not the same as being unwilling to make a contribution. He was a stage designer by profession, and on the last evening of the session he made each of us a beautiful wreath for our heads.

41

It felt like a gift directly from the Greek gods.

Then there was the question of what a community was. If this feels like home, participants seemed to be saying, why can't I just do what I want? Joe would buy a crate of peaches, and before the next meal came round, they were all eaten. If it was their kitchen, why couldn't they just go to the fridge and eat whatever they liked?

We discussed this at a community meeting, and people agreed that this just didn't work. But the very next day, I found people sitting around drinking the cooking wine from the kitchen, and complaining that they didn't want to have work groups. I didn't know what to do.

I went away and thought about it carefully. Maybe they were right. Why have work? And in fact, why have community meetings, particularly if people weren't going to keep to their agreements? But then without work or community meetings, it wouldn't be a community.

And suddenly I realised that if this wasn't going to be a community, I didn't want to do it. I was not a hotel manager, and I didn't want to run a hotel with groups. As soon as I became clear in myself, the problems stopped.

But I came to realise that the term community was confusing. Participants might be having the experience of community, but they hadn't got together to share ideas and resources to create the community together. They had simply paid us for a holiday, albeit one that looked like a community.

It was not in fact their kitchen, and if they were asked to work, it was not as a source of cheap labour, but because this was a building block of the world we were offering them.

I came up with the term "symbolic community". We were providing the educational experience of community that would be transformative, and it was built out of a series of symbolic communication structures. It was not a "real" community.

As I began to understand this, I felt freer about making more aspects of the community symbolic rather than real. Most notably, we employed a team of people who were there permanently, including a coordinator, a cook, an assistant, that sort of thing, as well as an administrator or two in London. This meant that the work was symbolic, too, rather than being essential to the running of the place.

Now, work groups did enough work to feel that they were active members of a community rather than passive guests of an institution, but they didn't need to clean toilets or cook meals. They were more likely to set tables, prepare vegetables, sweep the courtyard, or water the plants. Some were disappointed about this, others relieved. Some took the opportunity to opt out altogether.

According to Joe, participants had never been the ones who kept the place going. He said that organising the cooking group was like creating a children's work project, and it would have been easier to do it himself.

Slowly but surely, the community meetings began to make fewer and fewer major decisions. We were no longer looking to the community to create the shape of the session. The shape was there, and the decisions were relatively minor.

As the Centre grew, we began to have three personal development groups running at a time. At first, people moved as a group from one leader to another over the two-week period. That way, the group as a whole worked with all three group leaders.

Eventually, we started having people sign up for one leader one week, and another leader the second week. This introduced an element of popularity competition which I had been trying to avoid with the previous structure. I discovered that getting people to sign up for my group depended on how I was feeling that day. I'd stand up and say "Come to my group. I do a bit of this and a bit of that." That worked when I was feeling particularly charismatic, and not otherwise. Eventually, developing a focus on imagery as my way of working enabled me to get past my "bit of this and bit of that" approach to presenting my course.

We came to understand that personal development was exciting and intense but a bit one-sided. We began to offer yoga in the mornings and to have a "community facilitator" to offer creative and fun activities in the afternoons and evenings. And on the last evening, we would have a "cabaret" in which people performed in whatever way they felt inspired to perform, to an extremely appreciative audience. I often had to reassure people, "If you've been afraid of public performance, this is a place where you could fall off the stage and still be applauded."

Changes were happening also on the physical level. The wild overgrown garden became a paved courtyard with a view. Theo, a participant whose day job was architect, offered to design a second floor for our house. He stayed on for a week or two and designed the beautiful space that became our main group room. We also built another room with a glass wall through which you had a wonderful view of hills and sea. This was at first my favourite group room, and eventually became our art room.

Our brochures changed along with the Zeitgeist. After the first typewritten and photocopied brochure of one A3 page folded over, we graduated to brown and oatmeal four-page brochures, A3 size, on heavy matt textured Conqueror paper which we thought was the height of luxury.

Given Yannis' journalistic background, they were designed to look like an alternative newspaper, with the actual programme on a folded sheet inside, and they often had humorous stories, sketches and cartoons. We never wanted to be too earnest.

Even more important, we didn't want to seem too commercial. It was not until 1985 that we risked having a shiny brochure in full colour. What would people say? No one seemed to mind, so we went on with our colour brochures.

As the years went on, personal development became less popular, and we branched out into other courses. Our most successful was Yannis' idea of offering the Writers' Lab. It was a time when it was just becoming accepted that creative writing can be taught. And indeed, the writing course tutors were so inspiring that they started quite a few participants on their path to be successful writers themselves.

From the beginning, the Writers' Lab attracted luminaries of the writing world, many of whom were household names. While famous psychotherapists in general wanted to be paid at levels we couldn't dream of, famous writers seemed to be willing to come because it sounded like fun. And they loved being part of a team, and being treated in a simple open way by people rather than with the kind of famous person projections that normally limited their relationships.

The absolute importance of being treated in an honest, respectful, and loving way was true for everyone who came – participants, teaching staff, and permanent staff alike.

A Skyros participant from our second summer told me that the holiday was the best she'd ever had, and that she'd laughed more than she ever did before or since, and it had also completely changed her life, including starting her on the path to become a psychotherapist. When I asked her what about Skyros had made her new life possible, she told me that when she came there, a housewife and mother with almost no qualifications, she felt herself to be of no value. She came away feeling she was someone. That was enough to change everything.

A new set of mirrors made possible a new beginning.

In the background of all this, I was finding my way through the mirror of all the powerful projections on me, which I was completely unprepared for. I was in my early thirties, but I was the mother of a community of people, some of whom were old enough to be my grandparents.

Being the founder of a world, like being the mother of a child but more so, meant that you were the "be-all and the end-all", the centre of an archetypal myth. Whether I smiled at someone or didn't was a major event for them. If I cried, it just proved that I was so powerful I could afford to cry in public. When there was a crisis, I was the one who had to rise to it and lead the community.

The sessions were in two-week cycles, and each fortnight was such a total experience of a world coming into being and then dissolving that it felt like a lifetime. I began to feel like an ancient being, living lifetime after lifetime.

There was a moment in a getting-to-know-each other session on the first night when I stood at the top of the stairs, and noticed that two of the new participants resembled a couple from the previous session who had met and gotten together with disastrous results. Now I saw this new pair begin to move towards each other across a crowded room.

Is this what the gods feel when history starts to repeat itself?

Faced with the demands upon me to be wonderful, I did manage to rise to the occasion, particularly at moments of crisis. The Greater Dina was a lot bigger, more powerful, and wiser than I was. But on another level, I was still an awkward, insecure, needy child.

While the adult/ancient being was taking care of everyone and everything, the child within me was left to cope on her own, desperately trying to be a good girl.

I moved through various phases of my relationship to this role I was playing. Sometimes I slipped into an altered space, feeling like an ancient queen or goddess. Then I'd start feeling isolated and depressed and feel it was all projection, all unreal. None of it was real love, and I was completely alone. It took time for the swings to settle down, so that I could find a stable sense of the relationship between my personal self and my role in the community.

I had an enormous amount of power in that little world, but I wasn't looking for power, except the creative power of being a midwife for transformation. The little girl in me just wanted to be loved.

I remember my friend Sue, who was also a group leader on the staff team, saying to me, "I can't be unaffected by the fact that you are the Director here." I was devastated. Did this mean I couldn't have friends here?

"Then I give up" I said. "If you can't, who can?"

She said, "Don't give up. The point is, I'm working on it."

And for my part, I figured out that being a therapist did not mean that I wasn't allowed to have needs. There was a distinct moment when I realised that I too could reach out for help. I could feel my arms extending and had a sense that I did not need to be so alone.

Skyros eventually gave back to me what it gave to others and more, I felt valued and loved both for my contribution and for myself and I got a profound sense of contentment from the creative pleasure of this wondrous venture.

And as I learned to reach out, I found real friends, who could care for and protect me, who were not envious of me, who could accept that I was both strong and vulnerable. Many of them cared about Skyros almost as much as I did.

I was no longer alone backstage. I had my own community.

III. Atsitsa: Beginning Again

Prince Charles was present at the birth of our second centre, Atsitsa. He is not aware of this. Yannis is sitting in Skyros reading a newspaper account of Prince Charles' famous speech on complementary medicine. As Yannis reads about the balance of mind, body and spirit, he keeps feeling that this is familiar to him in a way that all our psychological work is not. It sounds almost Greek.

But of course, it is Greek. It is the ancient Greek approach to health.

Yannis turned to me, of course. Would I help him start a second centre with the principle of holistic health? No, I wouldn't. Enough was enough.

Fatefully, one of the participants, Clark, seeing how exhausted I was, offered to take care of my kids while I went over to Atsitsa to rest for a few days. I camped on a concrete slab in front of the taverna. Didn't they have rooms? I didn't think to ask. Pay for a room? I still hadn't left my sixties mentality behind.

I was so very worn out that my image of myself was of a tree reaching down into the parched earth, unable to reach water. There also happened to be an infestation of wasps that summer. I'd try to eat a watermelon and it'd be covered with wasps. I felt as if I was being chased by the furies. I just didn't have the energy to deal with them.

After two days in Atsitsa, I had a profound sense of the healing spirit of

46

the earth and sea. By the third morning, I could sense that the roots of that inner tree had pushed down and had finally reached water. As I looked at the wasps now, I was no longer frightened. After all, I was bigger than they were.

Returning to the Skyros Centre refreshed, and a bit in love with Atsitsa, I began to take Yannis' idea seriously. I sensed the possibility that Atsitsa would attract people who were not in my rarefied psychological world, and yet could benefit from the healing environment, the community spirit and the courses that we had to offer.

When we had started Skyros Centre, I had a kind of unconscious template in mind, coming as it did out of psychology and community traditions I knew well. This time we were trying to start a holistic centre, without fully knowing what 'holistic' meant, and what we were about to do. The concept of holistic medicine was just beginning to become known, and we were trying to do something even more unheard of – to create a holistic way of living.

Once again, we were pioneers and didn't know it.

We never considered doing market research to see if this was what people wanted. How can you ask people if they want something, when that something is evolving, and needs time to become what it is meant to become? Instead, we assumed that you need to get a sense of what you feel inspired to offer, do some research into it, and then put it out there. You hope others will get on board. More than that, you assume they will.

You just need to let them know how to find you.

On New Year's Eve, 1983/84, we invited everyone who had ever been to Skyros to an all-night party at our new home. The house was packed, and parking was a serious problem, but it was a great success and the first of many.

Then we put out our first Atsitsa brochure, calling it the Atsitsa Club. This was the last year of our brown and oatmeal newspaper type brochure, before we turned to colour, and it had the spoof headline: "No war games? Count me out," says President Reagan. "If only Achilles had never left Skyros…he might still be alive," weeps his sea goddess mother.

I was to spend our first summer in Atsitsa trying to discover what Atsitsa was meant to be, and how to construct a programme that would make that happen. I say "discover" because with a few new factors – the holistic focus, the location by the sea rather than in the village, the potential size – a rather different world might emerge than at the Skyros Centre, and we had to find out what that world would look like.

Summer 1984, and Atsitsa was launched.

Atsitsa was in an undeveloped bay, and people stayed in bamboo huts or in the house, mainly in shared accommodation, minutes from the sea, but miles from the village. There were two tavernas and a few houses nearby, but that was it. We didn't even have a telephone and it took ages to get allocated one. To make a phone call, you had to go to one of the tavernas, and sit in a queue to wait to use the phone presided over by the rather ancient Kyria Anna who spoke no English and sat there watching you speak as she banged her big fly swatter on the table.

Our intention in Atsitsa, just as in Skyros Centre, was to create a world that heals. As always, I knew this needed to begin with a sense of community. We had the community meetings, the courses, and the co-listening, as well as the Demos and work groups in the morning, swimming and sunbathing in the afternoon, and evenings of parties, special events and cabarets.

And yet Atsitsa was obviously quite a different animal than the Skyros Centre. This was not a personal development holiday but a holistic holiday which addressed the health of the whole person – mind, emotion, body and spirit. So we had a very wide range of courses, from windsurfing and swimming, to yoga and t'ai chi, to theatre, music, art and voicework, to meditation and psychological courses.

Rather than taking one main course for two weeks, plus various drop-in activities, in Atsitsa you had three courses a day, and you could change them each week. You could be doing early morning yoga or t'ai chi, late morning windsurfing, and late afternoon music in the first week, and early morning meditation, late morning personal development, and late afternoon theatre improvisation the second week. Or you could skip it all and hang around in the sun. Few people did, because the courses were so enticing. But by the second week people often opted for fewer courses and more sunbathing and chatting with their new friends.

All the courses were focused not just on that particular skill, but on the development of the whole person. And there was no telling which was the best route of transformation for whom.

Sometimes we went too far on the holistic focus. In the early days, when we taught windsurfing, we invited teaching staff who had expertise in what is called "The Inner Game", an approach to learning sport from the inside out. Unfortunately, those teaching the inner game of windsurfing at Atsitsa had a great approach to teaching, but very little idea how to windsurf.

Some of the participants loved it. Others got incredibly frustrated, saying that they just wanted to be taught how to turn the windsurf board around.

Because people took a number of different courses with different group members, they got to know more people, but they didn't have a stable connection with one group as in the Skyros Centre. We evolved the *Oekos* or home group, *oekos* being Greek for home. It was a bit like co-listening in a group, and it served as a safety net in the community, as well as being a way to focus with a small consistent group of people on what was important.

The wide range of courses to dip into meant that people could ostensibly come for one thing and end up doing another. A typical comment, particularly from the men, was "I only came for the windsurfing." The fact that they ended up doing meditation in the morning and self-esteem development in the afternoon was a bonus, and probably could be kept secret from their friends back home.

For me, it was the more physical sports that were more challenging, and a greater learning experience. I don't mind getting up in a group and showing all my feelings. This feels quite comfortable and normal to me. Standing up on a windsurf board is another matter. Just to believe that I am the kind of person who can windsurf requires an identity transformation.

I got as far in windsurfing as to have a photo taken of me standing up on the board to impress my kids. I even tried out abseiling, though I was terrified and almost went right back down the way I came up rather than step off the cliff as everyone else was doing.

Once I did it, however, I found how amazing an experience it was to walk down a rock face as if you were horizontal, held safely by ropes tied to the earth and to your teacher. I immediately translated the experience into a psychological approach in my courses. But after that one short course, I was glad never to have to abseil again. No new career there.

It was learning how to swim that made the biggest difference in my life. For one whole summer, I attended every swimming class, until by the end of the summer I could do the breaststroke well enough to get somewhere. As I swam around the promontory of Atsitsa towards the shore, I experienced the kind of exhilaration that I would previously have associated with a profound spiritual experience. Indeed, it was a profound spiritual experience.

And nowadays when I am in Atsitsa, my swim to what I call Emerald Isle, the little rock island in the bay, is a daily practice. If I haven't done it, I haven't had a day.

Not surprisingly, given our way of doing things, we had extraordinary teachers, great food, a seriously committed and helpful staff, and an amazing programme, but the place itself was nowhere near ready. The first session was completely crazy, with rooms and huts in the process of being completed, and people being moved from room to room as the work got done.

Did the participants complain? No, they thought they were in paradise.

After all, they were in a beautiful bay, between pine trees and sea, enjoying the company of wonderful people, taking courses from world-class teachers, eating delicious meals and having exciting conversations, parties and midnight swims. Of course they were happy, or so I thought.

What I didn't see was that once again, the first session was attracting pioneering types who love to come to a new venture, and are willing to put up with inconveniences and constant moves because the spirit of the place makes it worth it. Not everyone would feel the same way.

Our beginners luck had ended at the Skyros Centre in the second summer. Here it ended by the second session. Things were so improved that we expected a delightfully happy group. Then they arrived and we heard shocked whispers that it wasn't what they expected. We waited to hear how this beautiful place was so much more than they had hoped. But, no.

"Where are the tennis courts?" they asked.

It was our fault, I guess, given that in our desire to sound trendy, we had called it the Atsitsa Club.

Same beautiful bay, same wonderful courses and participants, same midnight swims, very different group.

The group split into the faithful pro-Atsitsa zealots, and the anti-Atsitsa zealots. The arguments continued until the very last day of the session. Not paradise, no. But this passionate debate contributed as much to Atsitsa as the halcyon first session.

Some complaints inspired wonderful debates in Demos breakfast meetings. People who had thought that living in nature would be quiet and peaceful complained about all the animal noises. The big question in Demos became: "What should we do about the cockerels that wake people in the morning?"

"Get rid of them," said one group. "They belong here and it is up to us to get used to them," said the other. "If you want to get rid of them, then you should be willing to kill them yourselves", argued a third group.

Eventually we rounded the cockerels up and sent them on a holiday to a neighbour who was happy to have them for the summer.

50

It was not just the lack of tennis courts and the presence of cockerels that were the problem in our paradise. The natural world, so beautiful and so healing, was our biggest asset at Atsitsa, but it was also our biggest challenge. Atsitsa was an exciting and joyful place from the beginning, with the same potential for transforming people's lives as the Skyros Centre. We knew how to create that wonderful atmosphere. But we didn't understand the new difficulties we were going to face in the lap of nature. Put simply, when you are not in a village or a town, you have to provide everything from water to electricity to a sewage system.

Yannis and I, used as we were to New York, Athens and London, were not prepared for this.

We discovered that every machine you have can go wrong – and will, particularly if your handyman neglects to put in oil, or proceeds to dismantle it and lay the bits out in rows without the slightest idea how to fix them, as was sometimes the case in the early days.

Most important, we relied on a generator to run the place, including pumping water from the well, so that when it occasionally broke down, everything from electricity to running water came to a standstill. People improvised with devices constructed from buckets or whatever they could find to create showers for themselves. Some loved it. Others, of course, did not.

We began to need a large permanent staff. The days of my being the first port of call were long gone now, and we seriously needed a structure to meet all the needs of the site as well as of the participants and staff. Managers like Niko Sikkes, Pam Chaplin, Julian Colborn and Pete Webb were brilliant at taking charge of this sprawling monster, a feat that was completely beyond my understanding. We also created a team of "work scholars" young people who came to work as well as take courses and be part of the community.

Being in a rather isolated world as we were, if someone became ill or became mentally unstable, we had to be thrown back on our own resources, at least until we could get to the clinic in town. At first, every alternative practitioner in the place would crowd around and prescribe something different. Eventually we decided to have a nurse who took charge of physical illness.

Where the illness was emotional, it was usually the therapist on site who was consulted. But not always. Writer Sue Townsend talked to me about what she did when a group member who became quite paranoid, was disrupting the group with his accusations and suspicions. With her usual panache she confided in him that she had a crime that needed solving and sent him off to Athens to do some research. By the time he returned, he was much improved.

While the backdrop of Skyros Centre was Greek village life, here it was the beautiful and rather wild natural world. We ate three meals together in the open-air dining room. Courses were normally held in the big outdoor circles with views of the mountains and the sea. But they might also be held in the threshing circle, or in a cave, or in a fishermen's chapel by the sea, or on the promontory facing us, or in the sea.

Participants and staff alike fell in love with the beauty of the place and the warmth of the atmosphere. Many people have told me than when they are imagining going to a beautiful and safe space in their meditations, they find themselves sitting on the promontory of Atsitsa, looking out at the sea.

Skyros Centre and Atsitsa became a bit like two competing neighbouring tribes. We used to have visits between Skyros Centre and Atsitsa, some walking and some going by coach, and participants of each centre thought their own was the best by far.

Each centre's participants thought the other centre was claustrophobic. The Atsitsa people thought Skyros Centre was claustrophobic because everything happened on that small terrace while Atsitsa had the big outdoors. The Skyros Centre thought Atsitsa was claustrophobic because they were together all day in the same location, rather than spilling out in the village.

Atsitsa people thought Skyros Centre people cried all day. The Skyros Centre people thought Atsitsa people were superficial. And so it went. And if you moved back and forth between the two, as I did, but also many other staff and participants did, you seemed to adopt the point of the tribe you were in and forget how much you loved the other one.

At one point, someone suggested that when one group visited the other we should bring gifts as if to placate the neighbouring tribe. Someone else came up with the idea of washing the feet of the Skyros Centre participants who had walked to Atsitsa, and this became our ritual for a while. Once or twice, also, we had wonderful great dramas played out between the two centres; one was the great battle between the Trojans and the Greeks, a drama introduced and master-minded by therapist and writer Gaie Houston. Another great cross-island adventure, complete with Odysseus, Greek gods, terrible temptations, and a wise Sphinx, was put on by psychologist and author Dr. Richard Stevens.

Despite all the differences between the centres, on the last day, when people wrote their evaluation forms, their descriptions of what was important to them about the experience were almost identical. I have always believed that this was because it was the nature of the community that was the real healer.

Atsitsa became a second home for many participants and staff. They'd come back year and after year, one participant actually reserving a hut for the same weeks of August each year. Or they'd come on their birthday to be sure of a great day. Or they'd come once or twice and then thirty years later. Couples who'd met in Skyros sometimes returned to have their marriage ceremonies on the promontory. I remember a speech Yannis gave at one of these weddings, "Many marriages end on the rocks. This one is starting on the rocks."

A participant from Chicago brought his son and daughter, both single, and that session, there was a wonderful group of work scholars from Frome, Somerset, who dyed their hair red, and wandered around painting murals and beautiful designs on the stone circles in their spare time. The brother and sister participant fell in love with two of these work scholars. A double wedding ensued.

Years later, a young woman came to visit and told us she was the daughter of one of these couples. She could even say which hut she had been conceived in.

And at the other end of life, a number of participants and staff have asked for their ashes to be sprinkled in Atsitsa. I find this very moving.

The Skyros experience started to be the basis of television programmes, books, novels, short stories and poems, as well as press. The Yorkshire Television series First Tuesday did an hour long documentary about us, saying it was "almost like living your life in a fortnight." Writer DM Thomas wrote a book called *Lady with a Laptop* which was a spoof of Skyros. He kindly named the mad bumbling holiday centre in his book Skagathos Holidays [3], and made clear that the Skyros Centre on a nearby island was the real thing, and Ruth Rendell was teaching there (which unfortunately she never did.) Sue Townsend wrote a little Adrian Mole piece as an introduction to my book *Life Choices, Life Changes*. Jane Salvage wrote a history of the Skyros Holidays called *Skyros: Island of Dreams*. I began to hear of published poems and short stories, including in the New Yorker magazine, which referred to our holidays or were inspired by them.

We had found ourselves a place on the cultural map. Or rather, the cultural map had expanded to include us. Sometimes holidays are not just holidays. Like science fiction stories, they can give us a sense of what is possible. [3]

53

References

1. The Guardian online, 20 March 2008

2. Buettner Dan *The Blue Zones: Lessons for Living Longer From the People Who've Lived the Longest.* (Washington, DC : National Geographic, 2009); Dina Glouberman and Josee-Ann Cloutier, "Community as Holistic Healer on Health Holiday Retreats : The Case of Skyros," Chapter 13,pp.152-167, in Melanie Kay Smith and Laszlo Puczko (Eds) *The Routledge Handbook of Health Tourism* (NY: Routledge, 2017); *Okinawa Centenary Study: Centenarians* (2007) http.//www.okicent.org/cent.html

3. DM Thomas, *Lady with a Laptop* (London: Carroll and Graf,1996)

4. Jane Salvage, *Skyros: Island of Dreams* (Skyros Books, 2011)

Dina at The Skyros Centre, 1981

54

3. The Early Years

Dina with baby Ari, 1977, before the Skyros Centre opened its doors

In a traditional dress during the spring of her life

Innocent as the moonlight. The village before the arrival of tourism

56

A neighbour and locals wondering why they are being photographed

The Skyros Centre's neighbours. No time to work on their tan

An old village street, almost as old as time

A landlady's welcome in a place close to an old neighbourhood

A fisherman in the village's harbour

'Socrates' making cheese in the village

Yannis with Chloe in 1980 and Dina on the window surveying the country

Serenading Pillar's and Tom Feldberg's son at the Skyros Centre

60

Silke Ziehl back, 1979, and Manos Loizos, the Greek composer, at the SC

Easter time and the lamb is on the spit. Dina, Yorgos Evgenicos & Antonis

Ari Badaines and Dina discussing the merits of the bougatsa cake

Sylvia in the swing of things. Another SC participant on the beach

Crazy times right from the very beginning - a 1982 Skyros Centre group

Listening to the Skyros oracle. After a week in Skyros, she can fly high

63

Demonstrating our support of the islanders in their ferry dispute in the 1980s

David Swenson introduces the village children to yoga in 1994

64

Kirkpatrick Sale, a leading US environmentalist, joins Skyros

Women for Peace make their point in difficult times

Ari is captivated by Paul's singing

Chloe working on her piece of art in the garden of the Skyros Centre

66

with all my heart, soul and body
I want To thank The centre for having
put me in Touch with the reality of life,
and for having made me feel who
I really am instead of how the others
usually see me. IT has been a fantastic
unforgettable experience.
Muito Obrigado e um beijo muito especial
da vossa
Maria de Freitas Branco
Agosto dia 23 de 1981

Notes and sketches in The Skyros Centre's Reflections Book of the early years

When the door
is opened the light
can come in ....

Keith Aug '81

My Thought For Skyros
August 1982.

I have woven a thread into
the tapestry of life here —
and I have Taken so many
new shapes and colours into
my own.
What a journey it has
been - true joy, sorrow,
laughter, pain and a new
glimpse into the heights
and depths of living and living
So much like the sea of
unfathomable depth.
In this moment now I
want only to give a deep
and sincere thank you and
Take away with me a
stillness and inner knowledge
that this summer road
will always continue to
lighten my life.
Chris.

67

Dina and Yannis in 1984: facing the light from which dreams are woven

On a journey to new lands: a Skyrian design

69

Skyros emerged as accidentally as a poppy

4. In the Direction of Our Hopes

By Yannis Andricopoulos

I. On the Exploration Road

Skyros emerged as accidentally as a poppy and was as original as Boticelli's Birth of Venus. Well, not quite! But its impact was spectacular. The idea popped up one evening out of a bottle of wine that myself and Dina Glouberman, my wife at the time, shared with Bridget Towers, her university colleague. Dina, a lecturer and psychotherapist, could run her psychotherapeutic workshops on a Greek island, Bridget might run her sociology seminars, and I could contribute all my skills and knowledge of Greece to ensure their success. Simple.

Bridget dropped out soon, but Dina loved the idea. It was coming close to a dream she had been nourishing for some time: that of an intimate community under the sun. What also appealed to her was the expectation that the project would give me something which would take me off the streets of depression. Unemployed at the time, I was feeling as empty as a library without books.

From a personal point of view, everything until then had seemed to be going my way: a decent career in journalism, a Ph.D. in History, three published books, and two years' experience at the very top of international student politics as the head of the Greek National Union of Students (in exile). All I had to do was choose the flavor of the cream to top my cake. Man's infinite capacity for illusion had obviously not made headlines in my thinking as of yet. I still believed in both my own serendipitous stars and the benign nature of the universe. Still I could not get a full-time job.

Incidentally, that was at a time that the UK seemed to be disintegrating. The Labour government's very rigid prices and incomes policy to cap rampant inflation had eventually forced the unions to take up arms against it. The winter of discontent had arrived – I still remember the tabloids headlines about the mountains of rubbish piled high in the streets, and the grave diggers' refusal to bury the dead. Even ITV was forced to suspend many of its programmes – Coronation Street, among others, had to go on a long vacation.

Whatever state the UK was in, the bottom line, however, was that I could not get a job. Luck seemed to have deserted me as it deserted even its own temple in Alexandria, the temple of the goddess Tyche, which the Christians had turned into a tavern. Or, if you believe in this sort of thing, this was my punishment for a past life misdemeanour.

The Skyros idea, something like a butterfly among grey moths, immediately captured my imagination. If nothing else, I now at least had something interesting to look forward to. Moving with vertiginous speed to make up for lost time, I immediately surfed the airlines' schedules for the earliest flight to Athens. The thought that this might be the beginning of a venture to be celebrated almost a lifetime later never signalled its presence at the corner of anybody's eyes. We went for it, my own natural daredevilling overcoming Dina's natural cautiousness, in the same way we could have booked a holiday in Tenerife. Mercifully, innocence is not always an albatross.

Simplicity itself

Dina's roots were very different from mine, as were her interests. Having grown up in a left wing Jewish family in New York, she studied psychology in the radical Brandeis University, whose faculty included Abraham Maslow and Herbert Marcuse, before moving to London where she did her Ph.D. on Piaget's psychological theory, social class, entrepreneurship and much else. At the same time she was training in existential psychotherapy with RD Laing's Philadelphia Association. When Skyros was launched in 1979, she had a full-time job as a senior lecturer at Kingston Polytechnic, and had established herself as a therapist and group leader with a following of her own. Unlike me, she was good with people. Like Charlie Brown, I loved mankind but I was not always at ease with its constituents.

We also had a two-year old son, Ari, and a few-months old daughter, Chloe, to raise. In addition, Dina had to take care of me, an unemployed wreck. Yet she was happy to go ahead with the project, confident that our boat, steered by the birds of the open sea and powered by the winds of fate, would reach its destination. Had we failed, an Oscar Wilde character would be happy to talk again about 'the astounding stupidity of optimism'.

Dina approached Skyros from her own psychological and social perspective. Her ideas can be traced to the writings of people such as Carl Rogers, Abraham Maslow and Erich Fromm, leaders of the humanistic psychology movement that has its roots back in the 1960s. Looking for the good life outside of the parameters of the market economy, its technocratic culture, and the various social and professional functions, they all anchored their approach on the full development of each person's potential. The problem, as they saw it, was the fragmentation of personal identity, the alienation of individuals from their own nature and their transformation into abstract functional units. Self-actualization for Maslow was at the top of the individual's hierarchy of needs.

The Skyros Centre innovation was to take the application of this Humanistic Psychology concept, which the 'Me Decade' of the 1970s had degraded to self-absorption, from the individual's personal development to a social context – the personal development holiday community in the serene Skyros island environment. The idea was quite simple: transfer an education process, in this instance the personal development process, into a new environment free from the city's hassles and constraints, and, at the same time, give the holidays a new meaning which could be as rich as life itself.

Relaxed in the island's alluring, primordial world, people could unwind, take a good, deep and honest look at their lives, explore pain, fears, inhibitions and habits that are getting in the way of a more fulfilling life, understand, accept and respect themselves for what they are, relate to other people more openly, deeply and effectively, and, using their emotional intelligence, re-launch their life-long journey.

Myself, I had no interest whatsoever in inner invisibilities or intimate therapeutic communities in the sun or in the shade. Psychotherapy sounded like a euphemism for licensed self-indulgent wallowing. It was as alien to me as the wedding rites of the Shamans before the industrial revolution. I was, of course, aware that the time when people were born into a personal community had gone for good – what remains is only its image engraved in memory, like that of buses powered by steam engines. But I was also totally unfamiliar with the shadowy side of our existence and could not grasp the amplitude of the pain which seemingly successful professionals secretly carried.

Though still faithful to my prejudices, that was, however, the time I was able to make the first optimistic entry into my diary, forgotten and blank for ages, and got fully involved with the project. I toured the Greek islands until I found Skyros: a land of timeless elation, neglected by time, shy of foreigners and as innocent as the moonlight. I also identified the place that was to be our Centre: the old building under the orgulous and indomitable castle of King Lykomedes, overlooking the Aegean's azure-blue sea. At the turn of the century it used to be a school.

A lovely island

The island, full of ancient memories, captivated me as soon as I set foot on it. I was taken by its primordial nature, wild yet curvaceous and flowing, the pastel of its landscape, the scents of its mellow summer nights, the mellifluous breathing of the Aegean Sea in whose 'lustral waters Zeus himself once delighted'.

Its magic is everywhere: in the sunlight which penetrates 'directly to the soul (and) opens the doors and windows of the heart', the odour of the freshly baked bread, the fleshy figs soaking in the early morning's dew, the moist brown eyes of the Greeks. It is in the youthful energy of unfaltering eternity, the sculptured countryside caressed by the Graces, the olive trees with the wrinkles of generations and the rocks with the wisdom of all time. I could even see there the sea-nymphs there dancing naked in the diaphanous shroud of the golden sunset.

I loved the old village too. The castle above it, rebuilt by the Byzantine Greeks and reinforced by the Venetians, graces the town and embodies the proud spirit of its people. Sculpted back up on the hill for fear of pirates centuries ago, the village itself has narrow cobblestone streets paved with unhurried intimacy and wholesome humaneness. Its white cubic-style houses, a testament of the indestructible innocence of caught time, are shaded by grapevines and bougainvilleas playing voluptuously with the nuances of the glittering sunlight. In the square, the villagers, weathered by the lingering memories of the millennia, still watch the visitors from their future with amusement and wonder in amazement at what is in store for them.

I felt as if I had arrived at an integrated, unflappable world, at peace with itself, serene in its wisdom, as ethereal as a Turner painting yet as solid and nurturing as Mother Earth.

As I sat on a stone, a surviving vestige of what was once a Homerian wall, I let my imagination glide back in time and acquaint itself with the shadows of the past. There, in front of me, were children of the prehistoric era playing games, Achilles, Odysseus, Nestor and Ajax, glorious Theseus telling King Lykomedes all about the dreadful Minotaur of Crete, and Athenian Kimon ferociously arguing with the surly and fierce Skyrians. There, too, were Byzantine priests urging their flock to repent before God lost patience with their sinful lot, Venetian sailors and Algerian pirates carrying on their back flagons of wine and young women, Ottoman officials, obese, debauched and drowsy, and coltish kids Mussolini had sent to conquer the world.

And then, Nicos Pavlis, our future Skyros Centre neighbour, passes in front of me on his donkey, with his goats and a friendly smile on his sun-hardened, lined face. '*Kalimera*', he says and offers me a bunch of red grapes. I recall Democritus, the father of the theory of atomism: 'Enough,' he said, 'is as good as a feast... True riches are found only in contentment.'

And, Oh God, I had more than enough. The odoriferous grapes, the convivial smile, the sensual delights of nature's breathtaking pastiche, the simplicity of life and the ancient breath of every stone had all engulfed me in a cloud of spiritual bliss. They had penetrated my soul and attuned me to the eternal rhythms of life.

Without even knowing it, I was on a spiritual journey. I listened to the whispering of the sea and I became that whispering. I absorbed the fragrance of the jasmine and I became the fragrance itself. I watched the eagles flying over the mountains and I became a proud high-flying bird circling the sky with them. I had extended myself spatially and diachronically, being what my eyes could embrace and what my psyche could trace in the fragmented memories of the mythical and more recent past. I felt part of it all, humbled in reverence, ennobled by the experience, mesmerised by and grateful for the beauty revealing itself in all its simplicity.

So far, so good. But there were also lots of practical issues to take care of such as deciding what to do with the building and coming to a satisfactory arrangement with the builders. All was done in good time, the building was quickly renovated and in July of 1979 it was ready to receive its very first visitors. Or almost ready; it was still receiving the finishing touches as we arrived – the fitting of windows and doors, for example. 'Thankfully', I thought later, 'the litigation culture had not taken root as of yet'.

'The English villa'

Known in Skyros village as 'The English Villa', a term which had an automatically sinister connotation as mysterious forces are at work and egregious things happen as a matter of course in English villas, the Skyros Centre was now a dream with blood in its veins. Neither Dina nor much less myself had, however, any notion of what we were starting. The venture was a journey into the unknown, stranger than fiction because fictional events have templates and precedents. Given that its website never gives you enough information, reality always takes you by surprise.

The programme, under the direction of Dina, was based on creating a community atmosphere through the personal development courses which used techniques such as psychodrama, Gestalt, bodywork, encounter, bioenergetics, art therapy and guided visualisation. Whatever the labels, I was impressed with their effectiveness in helping people to get in touch with their deepest selves, express their genuine feelings instead of their imitations, and bring their subliminal energy into harmony with their conscious awareness and choices.

Incomprehensible within the retail price index, such a process requires the guts to be 'you', the 'real you' as opposed to a 'you' conditioned by the requirements of socially determined patterns of behaviour. And then, of course, identity, often confused, mistaken, wounded, assumed, swapped, stolen, is anything but clear.

Further, to 'know thyself', as the Delphic maxims inscribed in the forecourt of the temple of Apollo at Delphi urge us, requires the disarming of the inner defensive mechanisms which block unconscious contact with one's 'real' self and one's 'real' needs. Hence there is an immediate conflict with the self-preservation impulse and the inhibitions activated by tiresome routines and all the demands of everyday life. It also requires an understanding of our world as a network of human relations rather than structures and systems, and a sense of oneness with an environment in which people find everything of value in and through each other.

The walk into the garden of our existence to reconnect with life's fragrance, lost in the alienated world we inhabit, is therefore not something most people would easily go for. Burdened by the lumpy, enervating mundane, sunk into the dailiness of life or trapped, as one woman wrote, in 'the treadmill of 50 to 60 hour working weeks in a back-stabbing academic environment', most do not even think about what they really need in life. Yet in Skyros, encouraged as they are to get in touch with their gut feelings, question and challenge our culture's assumptions and dauntlessly do what they need to do to lead a more fulfilling life, they do so eagerly and with an open heart.

Face to face with problems

Of course, as they do, they come face to face with the problems that shadow their lives: career or relationship problems, issues of health and sexuality, difficulties within the family, financial pressures or a range of bewildering choices that in today's world go far beyond those of the previous generations. Or with problems, as Saki, the witty and mischievous Scottish writer, might say, related to men who probably know exactly what to do if they find a rogue elephant on a lady's croquet-lawn but are just hopeless with women.

76

I discovered the pain behind the mask and touched its textured face right from the very early stages of the Skyros Centre's life. The picture, in very plain clothes, emerged most clearly for me the day a guest, an established journalist whom I used to see often on television, had joined Dina's course in order to file a story for his London daily newspaper.

'I'm only here to observe', he said with the hapless expression of a spokesman for the emotionally deserted street of his middle age, 'as I have no problems whatsoever'. His hidden uncertainty only seemed to be cover for a deeper uncertainty which became evident only two hours later. It was then when he burst into tears, which he mopped with a handkerchief the size of a small tablecloth, and started walking around with a pair of dark glasses to hide his anguish. Dina and he agreed that he was not ready to deal with the issues that came up and she counselled him off the course. He accepted it without protest and then surrendered himself to the pleasant lassitude of the afternoon idleness.

The issues that come up in this context are sometimes quite dramatic. A German doctor, for example, could not practise his trade because he did not want to inflict any pain on his patients. 'We Germans,' he said, 'have caused so much pain in the world that I don't want to add to it, even if it's for healing purposes.'

Other people had to deal with broken marriages, family splits, low self-esteem, feelings of social inadequacy, excessive burdens of family responsibility, loneliness combined with an inability to sustain new relationships, emotional vacuums, failed plans and expectations, sexual abuse during childhood or feelings of being stuck in a world where they did not feel they belonged. A woman even complained, while drying her hair in the sunlight, that she felt neglected because her husband never hit her back.

Others raised issues related to a work-life balance, and questioned their commitment to a career that deprived them of all else life can offer. What all these people, most of whom were going round the Middle Age Cape, really wanted was the opportunity to stand back, review their lives, seek new ideas and insights and get all the support they needed to change their trajectory through life's mountainous path. They did so, happily, or at least tried to, in a place which had just created within a day a real, not contrived, atmosphere that exuded warmth, friendship, camaraderie and a feeling of unbridled joy and hilarity.

Brought together by the universal language of the heart, what they were experiencing was indeed so extraordinary that I could hardly believe

I had witnessed it. It was even less possible to describe it to friends and acquaintances back home in London.

Help readily available

Skyros soon flourished as a personal transformation centre reminiscent to me of Vienna which, in Freud's time, had been taken over by the power of the unconscious. Still, at least at the very beginning, this did not reflect my own interests particularly as the tranquil environment was often disturbed by the unleashing of primal screams, presumably a part of the participants' uplifting downfall.

Unacquainted with such therapeutic techniques, the neighbours too wasted no time in reaching the conclusion that what had been established on their island was either a torture chamber, a mental home or a sadomasochistic clinic. It was quite funny, particularly at times when, in their kindness, they bravely rushed in to save the 'victims'. 'Don't worry– it's all play,' we re-assured them. 'A kind of theatre.' 'Oh good. When are you going to perform?'

At the end, there had to be an impromptu, if somewhat incongruous performance in Brooke Square, high above the village, in front of three hundred breathless villagers and Costis Ftoulis, their befuddled and mystified mayor. Surprisingly, the show turned out to be something of an occasion made possible thanks to my grotesque optimism and the creativity of the group. We did not become honorary citizens of Skyros, but the locals needed some time to recover. That was the first ever Skyros cabaret, the predecessor to those which have rounded off virtually every session since.

Yet, despite the phenomenal success of the new venture and my respect for its work, my connection with the Skyros Centre somehow remained peripheral. Unfamiliar initially with its concepts, I could not get involved with the self-realisation process. My slice of bread looked as though it was buttered on the wrong side. But as time went on, I did re-build my thinking and re-positioned myself vis-à-vis the unresolved issues of our time. As a result, new ideas emerged, founded basically on the belief that the boundaries between the personal and the impersonal had to be redrawn. Skyros had influenced my thinking perhaps as much as I, in time, influenced its own. 'Life is so queer,' P.G. Woodhouse once observed. 'So unlike anything else.'

All credit for Skyros, as it initially developed, therefore goes to Dina. She was the visionary, the soul of the community, its guiding spirit. She had a profound understanding of people, was bursting with positive energy, stuck to principles, and she had the right gut feeling about the way things ought to be going.

In search of a 'model'

As André Gorz, the Austrian social philosopher and a theorist of the New Left in the 1960s and the 1970s, pointed out, the unacknowledged mission of education is not to prepare all-rounded individuals, but to provide industry, commerce, the established professions and the state with workers, consumers, patients and clients willing to accept the roles assigned to them. The postmodernists likewise proclaimed the evanishment of the individual as a reflective, responsible and creative agent. The 'all-sided' individual, whom Marx referred to as 'integral' because his or her capabilities had been fully developed, could never be anything but a fugitive if the system did not stop producing individuals with an exchange value in the marketplace.

Psychology, I felt at that point, had to develop its political and social side to express the rebellion against the culture that stifles the individuality that it is trying to restore. But this is what modern psychology sometimes avoids like a headwaiter avoids the eyes of the customers.

The challenge for me was the creation of a world which would confront and defy this prevalent set of ideas and affirm the power of each human being against a hostile environment. What I needed was to turn abstractions, the infinitude of the ideas several of which had been dormant for ages, and also dreams, those woven in Skyros' exuberant light, into something I could touch with my fingers.

Thoughts were flowing through my head, but I had no model to build upon. The dream with all the élan and elegance of large gestures captured had to be re-dreamt. To this I am somehow indebted to Prince Charles, who in December 1982, a couple of years before Atsitsa raised the flag of holism, gave a speech in which he criticised modern medicine. By concentrating on smaller and smaller fragments of the body, medicine, he said, has lost sight of the patient as a whole human being. I can still vividly recall my instant reaction to it – fascination. The rest of Charles' speech did not enamour me – Paracelsus, the sixteenth century alchemist whom the Prince quoted extensively in support of his point is not my cup of tea.

But Charles' lecture reminded me of Hippocrates, the father of medicine, who would not treat a symptom without a full examination of the patient's whole condition which even included the political system of the city-state. This was not, however, just Hippocrates. The entire Greek culture was based on the same holistic premise which I proceeded to explore anew, as my education had left embarrassing gaps. The exercise soon highlighted what had taken residence in obscurity's back alleys. The holistic concept which unfolded was one in which unity enhanced diversity, purpose underpinned freedom, and wholeness strengthened individuality. The whole of the Greeks was more than the sum of its parts.

But conceptually speaking, we had to start from scratch as at the time, there was nothing to guide us, no precedent from which we could at least draw inspiration. The concept of holism, as of yet, had not moved outside the premises of alternative medicine. St Benedict's communes created in the chaos that followed the collapse of the Roman Empire were not really appropriate for our purposes, and the hippy communes seemed to offer a disincentive rather than encouragement.

But, although we did not know what the structures would be, we knew that it would be a community based on principles, commitment and integrity. Simplicity, openness and trust, honesty, acceptance and self-acceptance, non-competitiveness and mutual support, loving concern for each member of the community and respect for our differences were to be the beating heart of the new venture which was, moreover, designed to accommodate different schools of thought, ensure pluralism in action, and rely on principles rather than rules or dogmas.

Areté's 'lean, boyish body'

The holistic approach which Prince Charles reminded me of demanded the honouring of all our constituent parts – mind, body and spirit – and perfection through the development of personal human qualities embracing the whole of a person's existence. None of them were tradable against other goods such as wealth. The goal was the attainment of areté, whose 'lean, boyish body', caught by poet Odysseus Elytis' eyes of the soul, was the image of physical, moral and intellectual excellence. Articulating what Michel Foucault, the French philosopher, called the 'art of existence', areté demands the unappeasable love of beauty, from the beauty of the noble soul to the beauty of the institutions of a just society. It is indispensable to the happiness of the individual, his or her eudaimonia, and the re-establishment of a high trust society.

For the Greeks, the source of my inspiration, this was not the theory, but the everyday practice. The gymnasiums, where health and fitness were cultivated, were also centres for cultural activities and mental exercises. Alongside the athletic contests, the programme of the Olympic Games likewise included music competitions, prayers and rituals, communal singing, orations by distinguished philosophers and recitals by poets and historians.

80

Illness, like health, was likewise viewed holistically – Hippocrates, the father of medicine, always treated a problem within the context of the natural balance of the organism.

The goal was balance, proportion and symmetry, a life 'beautiful and honourable'. The concept is aesthetic, yet it required not only the beauty of the form, but also the beauty of the noble soul. It also precluded extremes of any kind, whether in the form of food fads or of religious excesses. 'A pure worshipper of the virgin hunt goddess Artemis,' Euripides said, 'is a tragic misfit.' The whole person should also honour the love goddess Aphrodite.

Holism also implied that the life of the individual was inseparable from the life of one's community, the polis. Self-rule was the norm and an Athenian citizen participated in all aspects of government activity. The polis, in return, was not just expected to run its business efficiently, but also to stimulate the intellect and satisfy the spiritual aspirations of its citizens.

The concept, I must say, developed gradually and at the beginning, in 1984, I often felt cornered by people asking me questions I could not answer as I wished. But it did develop, pre-emptying inter-alia theories that arrived together with the 21st century. The stunningly beautiful pine-forested Atsitsa Bay, the land, as Nietzsche would say, beyond all known lands and corners of the ideal, was the perfect place for it.

The location is, indeed, spectacular and the allure of its bay, cuddled tenderly by the breath of the pine forest, bewitching. The sea, though as old as time, has a face as smooth as a baby's. And peace, with a book on her side, sleeps on serenity's commodious bed.

Like a sunflower

Holism in the initial Greek sense has, however, disappeared into the mists of history. Christianity abandoned life on earth, and together with it the Greek holistic thinking for the pleasures of the afterlife guaranteed by the purity of the soul. The mind was dismissed, Reason rejected, the body denied and morality was identified with the denial of the flesh. Capitalism, a system which has never fought, and never will fight for heaven, subsequently rediscovered 'Reason' but as a weapon in its battle to turn everything into a means to an end which has always been associated with profit.

In its Cartesian world, the only important part of ourselves is the mind – the rest, i.e. the body and the soul, are burdens we have no choice but to carry. The concept of holism re-surfaced later on, but without the moral and ethical values with which the Greeks had underpinned it. The Romantics attached it to a totalitarian philosophy at the service of what Jean-Jacques Rousseau called the 'general will', and the New Age, like the Gnostics in the past, aloof to the traffic of this world, saw it again in metaphysical terms.

Distorted, misinterpreted or abused, holism has been deprived of its essence, detached from its ethical basis and rendered as meaningless as the remarks uttered by the spirits of the dead when we summon them to our presence. This is so even when lip service is paid to holism, when for example the fight against terrorism is linked to a new and fair world which only looks like the negative of a dream. Indeed, holism means nothing to the free market which is not interested in Justice but in wealth, has not set as its aim the happiness of the individual, for what matters is only his or her efficiency as a worker, and cares not about the well-being of the community. What matters is only its spending power.

The Greek holistic thought welded together Reason and morality, intellect and feeling, body and spirit, inner and outer, culture and nature, science and intuition, individuality and public realm. As parts of the whole, whether the whole was the planet, civilisation or the individual, they all had an intrinsic value, a purpose determined by their existence, and an inaliable right to be. As a result of all this, what was becoming clear in my thinking was that, whatever the political institutions and economic structures, what matters in our world is Justice, for Justice represents the whole of virtue, the essence of everything of value.

I became attached to this ethical understanding of holism, which shaped my political convictions, like a sunflower to the sun. Atsitsa is the evidence!

In the 'Wild West' of Skyros

Atsitsa, endearingly simple, was launched in 1984 in a way that looks hilarious in retrospect. Our brochure – an A3 sheet of paper – went out heavily tinted in my bizarre sense of humour. The contentious introductory paragraph read: 'President Reagan has let it be known that he does not intend to join Atsitsa, the holistic health and fitness centre on the lovely Greek island of Skyros. White House officials revealed last night that its summer holiday programme, which aims to revitalise the body, the mind and the spirit, is not exactly to his taste. "It does not include war games which the President loves to play", a close aide said'. Two months later we had to reprint it without any mention of President Reagan.

The initial public relations fiasco, however, did not prevent the successful launch of the operation, and this despite the immense physical difficulties that the venture had to deal with. Access to the building, located in the island's Wild West, through a treacherous roadway was a hazardous affair in the first few years, and all the things taken for granted in cities, i.e. mains electricity, running water, telephones or a sewage system, were all things of the dim and distant future. Some of them still are. In the first year, the outside toilets had no doors, the showers no curtains, and rumour had it that the first guests built their own huts. Guests who had come looking for tennis courts did, of course, complain.

Almost as troublesome were, and still are, other problems caused by the elements in the winter. Though the world has moved ahead since the old times, when to dance used to take two, nature has evidently not. It still remains stubbornly intransigent. The whole site has, as a result, to be completely revamped before the beginning of each season. Trouble, I often thought, is welcome in response to invitation. If not, it is as bad as kidney pain and often as expensive as privately performed brain surgery.

But usually, though not always, everything was taken in the best of spirits and the guests felt like pioneers. So did the members of staff, Silke Ziehl in particular, who helped enormously to turn the place into a wildly successful venture. In addition, self-discovery, creativity, camaraderie and often an outrageous sense of humour all contributed to an unforgettable experience which sang and danced its way into everybody's heart. Blending facts – naked midnight swims or summer solstice toga parties – with fantasies of thirty people to a bed, created, in the meantime, another focus for local modern mythology.

The courses offered in Atsitsa reflected its holistic approach to life as it had been epitomized by the Greeks and aimed at the all-sided development of the individual. Its very wide range of courses and activities included swimming, running, windsurfing, rock climbing, art, creative writing, music, theatre and movement, dance, mime and clowning, yoga, massage and naturopathic first aid, stress management, creative visualisation, dream interpretation, life choices and much more including talks on social and cultural issues and also politics. The sheer scale and variety of what was and still is on offer, someone wrote later, is 'an embarrassment of riches and a wealth of talent'.

I myself joined a few of these courses, but the one that most appealed to me was clowning, which, as it happened, was run by a beautiful Canadian with a seductive smile. I performed as a clown a few times in front of one hundred people, but I once chickened out and failed to do so. 'Sorry,' I explained, 'I can't stay as I've got to go to town to give a talk on the pleasures

83

of clowning.' Building dry stone walls in Atsitsa was also an undiluted pleasure. What I learnt I took with me to the Isle of Wight where, years later, I built a 15 metre-long garden staircase which I still eye with pride.

Not responding to the raw exuberance of the challenges Atsitsa posed was nearly impossible. In any case, I welcomed them as, allegiant to the spirit of my May 1968 days in Paris, I had to 'be realistic and demand the impossible'.

II. The Peerless Culture of Skyros

On a Skyros holiday you can stretch your muscles, start the novel you have been thinking about, create your own artistic masterpiece, join a comedy-improvisation workshop, sing your favourite songs or take a look at what you really need in life. The courses and activities available for the purpose include yoga, writing, art, photography, health & wellbeing, windsurfing, personal development, abseiling, trapeze, dance, music and singing and much, much more.

But courses are only one part of the many elements that turn Skyros into 'a magical' holiday resort [1]. The other part, which transforms the holiday into a landscape of hope and beauty, is its peerless culture. Within it, you can be yourself, reconnect with your essence, express your creativity, develop new skills, laugh as you have not since childhood and make new friends for life. More than thirty thousand people who have joined Skyros over the years, many of them numerous times, have done so and enjoyed the thrilling experience.

In the process, they relished its unbridled spirit of adventure, creativity and joy, explored new possibilities, tried new things and unearthed amazing layers of themselves they did not even suspect existed. Able to entertain themselves without help from the TV or the cyberspace, they also discovered parts of themselves that they did not expect to be there. In a world far removed from daily salaried routines, others took the opportunity to reassess their life, redefine their needs and re-set their priorities. The unexamined life, as Socrates said, is not worth living.

This Skyros culture is underpinned by an ethos that emphasises being rather than having, doing rather than consuming and belonging rather than withdrawing into the garden of your private world. Rather than resign, accept and conform, people are encouraged to question, challenge and create. Fulfilling our potential affirms what is best in ourselves. It also

84

asserts our power over our creations – the market, machines, technology, systems, fashion, ideologies or fundamentalist beliefs. Emphasis is also placed on cooperation rather than competition, participation rather than non-engagement, responsibility rather than indifference, respect for individuality rather than conformity, and support for the individuals' drive to unearth their dormant potential.

Seen in a wider context, this culture, central to the development of new, human-friendly social and political structures, brings together the personal and the political, which are two sides of the same coin. It is also what challenges the structures of our materialistic, consumerist and technocratic culture. In a very broad sense, it is all about inner and outer change, for the discomforts of our time are as much ill effects of our social values as the latter are ill effects of our individual perceptions.

This is in a way the working class culture revisited – a culture which, as expressed in Chartism, is based on mutual aid and cooperation. Opposed to it stand both the middle-class culture, based on rewards for individual success and the aristocratic ideal of hierarchy, grounded in birth and privilege.

This philosophical underpinning of the Skyros culture is developed and fine-tuned through an experiential practice that makes it work. Very often, as a result, people often return home with modified, and sometimes radicalised perceptions of both themselves and the world we live in. Life as it is lived is no longer viewed as destiny.

Some basic principles

Though simple is never simple, the principles on which this Skyros culture rests are fairly simple. People are first and foremost asked to be themselves. This is the key to an authentic life lost in the intricate, confusing social network of interconnecting pathways that often seem to require placing genuine feelings in the safe and display only their imitations. 'Which of us', Elisabeth in a JM Coetzee story asks rhetorically, 'is what he seems to be?' The problem here is, as Rachel says in a Virginia Woolf story, that 'nobody ever said a thing they meant, or even talked of a feeling they felt'. To be themselves, people would have to cast aside habitual roles, leave behind all features that make up their 'identity', and reconnect with their essence.

Though liberating, leaving behind the trappings of the 'real' world is, however, anything but easy. 'To be nobody but yourself in a world which is trying day and night to make you like everybody else', E. E. Cummings, the American poet and playwright, once said, 'is the hardest battle you will ever fight'. Hence people are encouraged not to sail under false colours, but, taking a risk, show instead their real selves in the certainty that they will be liked for what they really are. After all, they are reminded, we all have sides that we do not feel comfortable with and we are often uncharitable towards our own selves. Honesty, of course, demands courage.

People are also asked to give lovingly in terms of concern, time and attention to others as much as they can without expectations of getting something in return. Giving their best for the pleasure of giving, they can, incidentally, also be sure that the best will come back to them. As Democritus said, 'he who loves no one is loved by no one'. But they are also asked to accept what is being offered to them with appreciation and grace. Accepting is sometimes more difficult than giving.

People are further encouraged to give an outlet to their creativity and try things they have never tried before, from singing to abseiling, from comedy improvisation to painting, from windsurfing to writing, even if they do not feel comfortable or confident about it. After all, everybody is in the same boat. They are finally advised to reconnect with the child within – the child's curiosity, innocence, spontaneity, lack of fear and uncritical joy, and see everything as a world waiting to be discovered, a game to be enjoyed, an opportunity for a good laugh. Whatever one's age, playing is the salt of life. 'Play and don't worry about anything', I add when I am there. 'Or, at least, do not worry, as the Skyrians say, about two things in life: those that can be fixed and those that cannot.'

As it happens, in Skyros' honest and supporting environment, people who, if they had gone somewhere else, would have made certain that they had travelled as far away as possible from themselves, do listen and, as a rule, end up as happy as swallows in the spring. 'Every day', David Tillett, a member of the Skyros community, wrote, 'there is a fabulous journey, a possibility of magic, an opportunity to apprehend the glory of living'.

The Soul of Spring

Still, though everything appears settled, nothing actually is – the spirit of innovation has been ever-present. New ideas, whether spectacularly successful or dismally ill-conceived, flow in constantly and turn the place into the imagination's workshop. The leader in this instance is the Skyros community itself.

The community gives voice to its members, that 'intelligent, amusing lot – well read, on for a bit of crack, and not at all smarmy,' as Anne Roper put it in Ireland's *Sunday Independent* [2]. It enables them to influence the day's schedule, contribute to everybody's welfare and, in doing so, ensure people interact with each other as if they were a family – albeit without the usual family hindrances. Among them one could easily find his or her next door neighbour or, as Lynn Wallis wrote in the *Evening Standard* [3], people such as Lawrence Boswell, a theatre director who has worked with Madonna and Matt Damon.

People engage with the community through demos, the daily early morning meeting held for the exchange of news and views. Its importance rests not so much on the decisions it is occasionally asked to make, but on the genuine feeling it generates that people are consulted, listened to, counted for, respected for what they say, and able to influence the course of the day. The procedure transforms them into active members of the community, and also, in its own very small way, gives everyone a sense of the rights and the power they should have back in 'real' life.

Alongside it are the daily *Oekos* groups [4]. *Oekos* in Greek stands for home/family. In the Skyros context, it means a home base of like-minded people who interact with each other as if with a friend. Its members are accordingly open and honest about themselves and delighted to share with the group their fears, frustrations, hopes, expectations and dreams. Their open and honest lines of communication transcend age, class, sex, race and also professional and cultural biases and provide a unique forum in which people, free from the usual habitual restraining influences, can establish a most effective line of communication.

Oekos soon became an oasis of intimacy whose appeal spread all over the world, from the US to Russia. Several of them, years after they were formed, are still in existence. In some instances, they embrace an entire neighborhood as in the case of the Six Streets Group that emerged in Derby and, as Wendy Roberts wrote in *The Derby Telegraph*, had been going on for four years. Their Christmas party attracted 100 residents [5].

Love made visible

Co-listening [6], the third part of the communal structure, involves the same process as in *Oekos* but between two people only. On top of all this, and as the life of the individuals is inseparable from the life of their community, everybody is asked to perform a few communal chores. Chopping vegetables for lunch is one of them. Participation in these groups, which is voluntary, has occasionally been controversial as some people object to spending something like thirty minutes a day doing what people do not do on holiday. But convinced at the end that work is 'love made visible', they embrace it wholeheartedly.

One of them was Judith Linder who, as she wrote in *The Observer* [7], 'grew to love peeling onions' because it made it easy for her to bond with 'the lots of like-minded people'. 'Even the shyest members of the group,' Deirdre Mullins wrote likewise in the *Independent* [8], 'have no difficulty meeting others.' Work, after all, abolishes all social, age or gender differences, underpins the individual's sense of responsibility towards the entire community, our polis, and strengthens everybody's connections with everyone else. It is entertaining too, as it adds something to the palpable feeling of joy and hilarity.

Of key importance in all these activities is the establishment of an atmosphere of trust, which is what makes Skyros a safe place to be. Simplicity, openness and honesty, acceptance and self-acceptance, non-competitiveness and mutual support, loving concern for each member of the community and respect for our differences offer a pretty solid foundation for this. It is what acts as a catalyst that transforms people's perceptions, affects consciousness and opens the windows to the beauty of the world which adult life is keeping shut.

This broad and rather discernible intellectual construct places Skyros beyond the reach of any definition. It is also what puzzles me when I am asked to explain what it is all about. How can you describe the soul of spring? 'Well', I have said in a few such instances, 'it's all about living fully in the moment – and making the most of it. It's about the joy of living, if joy stands for something beyond the 'fun' offered to us by the entertainment industry. It's the pleasure of going for the spectacular which transcends every preceding fear, and the delight experienced by the appreciation of things for what they are – 'a river for its riverness', as Plato said – as opposed to their benefits in this life or the next. It's also a total living experience.

The 'Holistic Mecca'

Skyros, which *Elle* magazine wrote 'has become something of a Holistic Mecca' [9], is the present but also the future. It helps people to work out what they really need in life and set out on a whole new way forward. The question 'what would really make you happy?' seems very simple except that, if one tries to answer it honestly, it may well turn into a hand grenade exploding at the foundations of each one's existence.

The allure of a glamorous life can be as irresistible to some as saffron-robed Eosa's constant longing for young mortals. But overall what people believe they want is to be physically attractive, intellectually stimulating, professionally successful and also to lead a comfortable life in line with current expectations. Yet, to be happy they do not want more of the same, particularly if they gamble away their heart as a result.

Hence the answer is not a Lamborghini, but a safe space in which they can feel accepted, needed, valued and respected for what and who they are, a meaningful job that is socially validated, a sense of purpose that is larger than one's own self, and a world, their world, in which they feel they belong and to which they can relate. Important in this context is our living as human beings rather than functionaries or consumers, a simpler and more fulfilling life, and, of course, good, loving relationships. In short, a life that makes sense. It follows that in this world, 'more' means something different than what our materialistic, technocratic, consumer culture provides.

And this is what Skyros provides in the spirit of creativity, risk-taking and self-discovery. Still Skyros is not a school. It has no gurus to preach the 'truth', it espouses no dogmas, and it has no prefabricated interpretations of anything to offer. Its culture is, instead, underpinned, developed and fine-tuned only through an experiential practice to which everybody is invited to contribute.

Changing times

Meanwhile, as time went on, Skyros island developed a taste for tourism and the money it brings. Roads were sealed, hotels built, nightclubs and restaurants mushroomed and East European immigrants arrived. The Internet Café now electronically signposts the new era for the island. The locals changed too, as trends, like gravity, can only be resisted for so long. The young men frequent clubs rather than tavernas and drink whiskey rather than local wine. Young women, all graduates of the *Ecole des Femmes*, are as fashion-conscious as their counterparts in London's Knightsbridge. The old days when you would not dare even to enquire about the health of another man's wife had become the stuff of sitcom script-writers.

Yet the magic of the island has not dissipated into the thin air of globalism. A prejudiced pride in its past and a stubborn commitment to its Greekness would not make room for it. At any rate, an up-to-date unconscious cannot be acquired even if desired.

The Centres have also changed. The level of organisation and comforts simply had to rise from the laid-backness of the sixties. But the guests have also changed, though I still remember from 1984 that lady with an accent which made even the Queen sound rather plebeian. Rather than representing the fringes of society, guests now tend to be professionals, many of them leaders in their fields.

Yet the spirit of the place had not changed a bit as Skyros' soul had successfully resisted the market's designer spirituality. Anything different would have impoverished the richness of the experiences and robbed many people of their most treasured memories.

As strong has remained the connection of both Centres to the local community. This connection is based on respect for the local culture not as a matter of courtesy, but because of its intrinsic value. After all, unlike wealth, the gift of wisdom, just like light, is equally distributed amongst all peoples of the world, and the visitors can learn something from the sagacity of the locals. Special care is taken in this respect to honour the local traditions, and, very importantly in this sense, not to expect the locals to adjust their way of living to that of their visitors. The latter have graciously and wisely accepted that money cannot buy everything, including the respect and the friendship of the locals.

Skyros Holidays also regularly offers help to the Skyrians, particularly since the 2008 financial crisis hit Greece, to re-equip the local health centre, ensure the heating of all the local schools in the winter, help many families in distress and contribute towards the welfare of the local dogs, cats and also the Skyrian ponies, one of the rarest horse breeds in the world.

Equally important is, likewise, the two Centres' contribution to the cultural life of the island through concerts in the village *plateia*, exhibitions, street theatre events, yoga for the local children and also through the half-marathon Peter Webb and Kevin Whelan, members of the Atsitsa staff, organised each year with the participation of visitors and locals. I never joined this half-Marathon but I most definitely would have if it did not involve running.

The Education of Desire

Meanwhile, in 1992 another major step for the development of Skyros was taken when the Writers' Lab was established. It was once again a very innovative step: holiday writing courses within the Skyros community for people who were looking for inspiration and help to start, shape, develop and turn their ideas into a book. The new venture attracted many celebrities such as Sue Townsend, Margaret Drabble, Hanif Kureishi, Steven Berkoff or Hilary

90

Mantel. It was named by both *The Guardian* [10] or *The Age* of Melbourne [11] as 'No 1 of the World's Five Best Writing Holidays'. The *Independent* [12], likewise, saw it as a market leader in the creative-writing sector.

One of those I failed to persuade to join it was the Nobel prize winner Doris Lessing with whom I occasionally shared a coffee in West Hampstead where we both lived. John Mortimer declined the invitation too. Creative writing, he argued, could not be taught. My arguments to the contrary failed miserably to move him. I wonder, if he were still around, what would he have made of the creative writing courses run nowadays in almost every UK university.

Two years later, in 1994, we worked with another fifty Skyros people and launched in the UK a movement embodying the Skyros values. It was an *Oekos* movement, which soon spread to several other countries. Fifty or so *Oekos* groups sprang up in no time all along the UK and several of them functioned for years. 'We've survived weddings, divorces and even death, and we're still going on' I was told by a member of the Bristol group which had been meeting for ten years. They did so because, as others said, whatever you gained in Skyros, whether it is hope, confidence, renewed faith, camaraderie, new interests, ideas or skills, needs to be nurtured. So do friendships and the spirit of the Skyros community.

As the declaration adopted by the *Oekos* initiators stated, the idea was to bring the Skyros values into everyday life by bridging the gap between the ideal and the practical, and the temporary nature of the island experience with the more permanent demands of our living realities. The aim was to foster an individual sense of identity and empower people so that they could take charge of their own destiny, free, like seagulls over the sea, from oppressive and authoritarian structures.

As such, *Oekos* is not an organisation but a philosophical approach at the heart of which is what E.P. Thompson, the leading Marxist thinker whom I was happy to meet in Holland in the early 1980s, called 'the education of desire'. The aim, ultimately, is to bridge the gap between the personal and the social and, in the broadest sense, political, and speed up the pace towards a new society that values itself, its members and the natural world.

As such, it was in tune with a wider movement headed by people such as Murray Bookchin, the American political theorist, who was advocating the reinvigoration and the greening of our cities along with the development of an urban 'life place' consciousness. This is, indeed, what many people see in the Skyros community because, as Jane Salvage put it in her excellent

91

book *Skyros, Island of Dreams* [13], when they reflect on what makes Skyros so special, they almost inevitably think about what is wrong back home, in their own lives, communities, workplaces and society. 'Politicians and world leaders,' a participant had told her, 'might benefit from a fortnight in Skyros!'

The experience is, indeed, political, but neither in the context of party politics nor in the framework formed by special interests as represented by campaigns, societies, Rights' Associations, Trade Unions or NGOs. The latter only deal with a small portion of quantifiable concerns that make sense in the context of the institutions. They are useful insofar as they try, sometimes with some success, to correct imbalances in a disequilibrated world. But they cannot express the needs of the individual.

Politics, however, needs to embrace these concerns, connect to the fundamental condition of individual existence and engage with our times' cultural battles. The *#MeToo Campaign* today is the outstanding example of this. It is in this sense that the personal becomes political and the political personal. Inner and outer walk together hand in hand. People certainly create structures which can be good or bad, but being conditioned by them, they are also their creation.

'The New Game'

Skyros was founded on hope – the hope that one can be true to his or her own self within a world that makes sense. It is still travelling in the direction of that hope. Activities, as a result, thrive in the spirit of creativity, camaraderie, risk-taking, self-discovery, tears, laughter, craziness and a scintillating sense of humour. 'This is the name of the new game', Kate Birch wrote in *Aquarius* [14], a United Arab Emirates magazine, and 'Skyros is the epitome of it'.

But this 'new game' is also what provides the inspiration that has changed the life of many of the thousands of people who have joined Skyros over the years. One of them was Jimmy Carr, the comedian, who, interviewed by *The Sunday Times* [15], said: 'I have had one life-changing holiday – on the Greek island of Skyros... I had just given up my job with Shell. I wasn't quite sure what to do with my life, so I enrolled on a creative-writing course and learnt how to do massage, in the hope that something would occur to me. People kept saying that I was really funny and ought to be a comedian, so I thought I'd give it a go.' Jimmy Carr was anything but the exception.

Jennie Dempster, another Skyros participant, told as much to *Red* [16] magazine: 'I didn't really know who I was until I went on that holiday. If I hadn't gone I'd still be a TV producer'. Or Jackie Pilkington who praised 'the magic of Skyros' that changed her life. She was at that point, she told *The Daily Telegraph* [17], 'at a crucial crossroads with my marriage in shreds and a decision to make as to whether I scooped up my young son and dogs and went back to my home in South Africa.'

Skyros made a big difference for Judith Linder too. 'Going on the holiday', she wrote in *The Observer* [18] 'gave me the confidence to make some decisions. When I got back I moved jobs, moved flat and got my motorbike license. But the most rewarding aspect was the friends I made'.

I have so far and in a general way outlined the Skyros philosophy and the effects a break in Skyros has had on those who have joined it. In the next few chapters, the media, which was stuck at the traffic lights and could not join the conversation in full earlier, are given a chance to offer as briefly as possible their own views and assessments. They are both very interesting, particularly as they highlight aspects of the holiday experience I have not expanded on.

III. Through the Media's Eyes

As mentioned already, several publications have focused on the life-changing impact of a Skyros holiday. The transformation can indeed be dramatic, but in many cases it only involves a re-adjustment of one's priorities or perceptions. As Joan Scales wrote in *The Irish Times* [19], 'life hurtles by so fast that sometimes we want to say stop, get off the superhighway and breathe. There are times, too, we need to say stop, get off, and find some me time'. She found it in Skyros. So did Trudi Orchard, who, as she wrote in *Elle* magazine [20], 'I looked in the mirror and decided my eyes are beautiful. Something has definitely shifted in the way I see myself.' Or Sharon Garfinkel, who, writing in *The Jewish Chronicle* [21], stated that Skyros 'answered my prayers and gave me the ability to find what I needed'.

Change is, of course, anything but a must. As Leah Hellen wrote in *Top Santé* [21], 'I was just as happy to discover that I had it in me to feel good about myself'. So was Martin Hall, the fireman who arrived in Atsitsa as the 2005 winner of a BBC competition and loved the activities on offer. 'I was jiving on Monday night,' he wrote on his return to the UK, 'reading poetry on Tuesday, wine-tasting on Wednesday, performing as Robbie Williams on Thursday and dancing under the stars in the disco on Friday. And on top of this I had a singing course with a real pop star, a self-defence course with a four-times British champion, and sailing and windsurfing on the Aegean. Surely the magic of it, quite literally took my breath away. I had died and gone to heaven.' This was obviously much better for him than winning a free first-class railway pass for life.

But it is the transformation process that makes the headlines more often than not. 'To read Skyros press coverage', Kate Rew wrote in *The Observer* [22], 'is to choke on cliché: words like "life changing", "transforming". Yet at the end of two weeks, Skyros has been all these things.' The same was the case with *Huffington Post* [23] or with *The Age* [24], the Melbourne daily, whose writer stated that 'life changing' and 'transforming' are 'common testimonials'.

'People,' Lesley Garner wrote in *The Sunday Telegraph* [25], 'go to Club Med to forget themselves. At Atsitsa they hope to find themselves, or at least some interesting, new and undiscovered bit.' 'Skyros is not a superficial holiday experience that revolves around booze', Kate Weinberg added in the *Evening Standard* [26]. What 'enamoured' her was its community. Hence Hugo Williams, whom Janet Watts portrayed in *The Observer* [27] as 'the licensed sceptic of Skyros', in his column in *The Times Literary Supplement* [28], described Skyros as 'the holiday you can take home with you.' 'This is a lesson in uncynicism', Watts was then forced to confess!

High level of trust

But what *The Daily Telegraph* [29] called Skyros' 'fantastic breaks', is much more than that. It is great fun too – and fun, often wild and crazy, perhaps contributes as much as anything else to the rediscovery of life's meaning. 'Anyone can do anything,' Barbara Gunnell wrote in *The Observer* [30]. 'Age is irrelevant as I found myself sitting next to the "hooligans" so designated (by me) because of their iconoclasm about Atsitsa's more spiritual offerings. If Atsitsa was a pious place, the hooligans would have been miserable. But it wasn't'. Angela Neustatter was likewise taken, as she wrote in *The Times* [31], not only by Skyros' 'intellectual rigour and spiritual encounters' but also by 'the good old-fashioned rioting in the evening'.

Deb Hunt, writing in Sydney's *Sunday Telegraph* [32], enjoyed, too, 'the sort of fun you probably haven't had since you were a small kid', while Rebecca Taylor was taken by Skyros' boisterous daily life. 'I talked for England,' she wrote in *Time Out* [33], 'laughed, danced Zorba-like on the terrace as the sun set, reflected on life and the universe, boogied the night away in the local Music Bar and drank too much retsina'.

Something similar was mentioned by Jackie Pilkington in *The Daily*

Telegraph [34]: 'During this week,' she said, 'we soaked up the views of the wine-dark sea from the vine-covered terraces, over-indulged in seafood and salads and laughed as only one can if one is relaxed and happy'. Or by Melissa de Villiers who, as she wrote in *Red* magazine [35], was taken by the moonlight swims and the impromptu discos.

'It seems that,' Ailbhe Brilley wrote in *The Irish Times* [36], 'whatever way you sample Skyros, it has a huge impact, which is why people keep returning year after year.' A similar point was made by the Canadian newspaper *The Globe and Mail* [37] and by Roisin Ingle in *The Irish Times* [38]. 'Atsitsa,' Tracey Jennings wrote in *Health & Fitness* [39], 'is probably the perfect holiday. The joy of getting to know people whose ages and backgrounds were totally irrelevant, combined with the excitement of achieving goals and breaking old perceptions, made the experience all the more special... I'd never laughed so much or enjoyed such a range of emotions with such a great bunch of caring, supportive people. I returned rejuvenated, healthy, and more positive and with three new close friends.' As ITV's *First Tuesday* pointed out in its hour-long documentary on Skyros back in 1993 [40], 'it's almost like living your life in a fortnight'.

'The whole set up', an Oxford university scientist concluded some time ago, 'is unconventional, almost crazy. But that was a strength as far as I was concerned'. 'Its replenishing madness', author Steve Attridge likewise wrote, 'is something I have savoured long afterwards'. Woolfy, the Alsatian dog, which, having been brought up by the British Atsitsa community kept barking in Greek but with a foreign accent, agreed.

The Cabaret

The highlight of many people's experiences is, however, the famous cabaret at the end of every session to which nearly everybody contributes like an accomplished entertainer. 'The blossoming creativity is truly awe-inspiring,' Mary Comber wrote in *Health & Fitness* [41]. 'But it's only during the holiday climax, the famous Atsitsa cabaret, that we realise just how far we've come.' 'There were beautiful harmonies by the singing group,' Sharron Livingston wrote likewise in *The Travel Magazine* [42], comedy sketches, pieces of writing inspired by attendees of the writing class, poetry and of course, trapeze. It was truly uplifting to see how much could be achieved in just a few days.'

One of those who left proud of his achievement was Damian Barr, writer, columnist, and playwright. 'The diagnosis was made in childhood,' he wrote in *The Times* [43]. 'Never would I sing a song or so much as hum a ditty. I was, the best experts concluded, totally tone deaf. Until a holistic odyssey to the Greek island of Skyros.' In the Atsitsa cabaret Damian actually performed 'an ambitious solo'. 'I soar,' he wrote, 'to the snowy peaks of a previously unscaled vocal range. Greg wipes a tear, or possibly some dust, from his eye. "You are now," he says, before the assembled group, "a trainable tenor." Mentally, I polish my first gold disc. My voice healed, I fly home, singing to myself.'

The word 'madness', i.e., the incredibly high spirit in which people operate and which adds an unforgettable chapter to everyone's personal history, often appears in the description of the cabarets. I have myself witnessed or have been told of lots of such 'mad' events, though I, unfortunately, can no longer recall some of them as the fingertips of my memory cannot reach the shelf upon which they are stored.

People, as a result, *The Irish Times* [44] stressed, 'don't want to leave. 'I'll miss', its reporter added, 'our bamboo hut in the pine trees. The new friends, aged sixteen to sixty something. The sense of community. The sunsets. The shooting stars'. And of course the food, the 'wonderful traditional meals', which, author Michèle Roberts wrote enthusiastically in the *New Statesman* [45], 'the spiritual athletes wolfed'. People who have never been in Skyros often wonder if all of this is real. 'Yes, it is', Paul Mansfield reassured them in *The Sunday Telegraph* [46]. 'In fact, it's a hell of a lot more real than most people are used to'.

Making friends for life

A striking result of all this, Moyra Bremner wrote in *The Guardian* [47], is 'the creation of a climate that makes possible a meeting of minds in which the barriers of age and gender dissolve and people experience that rarest of treats – simply being valued for who they really are'. And these people, Claire Droney stated in *The Irish Examiner* [48] with reference to her own group, represent 'a diverse group of people, of all ages: lawyers, academics, teachers, photographers, psychoanalysts, psychologists, a yoga teacher, a theatre company director, an entrepreneur, a blogger, and a former glossy magazine editor. They are married, divorced, widowed, in love and successfully single'. Her feature in the newspaper had, incidentally, been given the title 'Letter from Paradise'.

Equally impressed, Crysse Morrison wrote in *The Times* [49]: 'What impressed me most was something more subtle, profound, and long-lasting –

96

the ethos of valuing both community and individuality, a way of being together that was inclusive, supportive and creative.' As a result, Andrea Anastasiou blogged [50], 'I found myself enjoying the company of every person I spoke to. There was no forced small talk. There were no fake niceties. Everyone was genuine and authentic. Hand on my heart, those were two of the most magical weeks of my life... These beautiful souls, who just two weeks previously were strangers, are now my friends.'

At the end, John Hargreaves wrote in *Here's Health* [51], 'you make friends for life'. 'I've made bonds that will last a lifetime', Anne Roper likewise stated in Ireland's *Sunday Independent* [52], 'and that was because the friendships were based on their getting to know the real me and vice versa'.

The atmosphere may provide, as Peta Heskell wrote in *The Guardian* [53], 'the ideal opportunity to put your flirting skills into action', but friendships have often led to marriages. That was the case of special-needs teacher Albie Godson and author and journalist Suzanne Power, who Andrea Smith tells us in the *Independent.ie* [54], fell in love with each other the moment they joined Sue Townsend's writers group. Noelle, likewise, who, as she told the *Cosmopolitan* [55], was proposed to by McElya while she was still in Atsitsa, had a wedding service on the Atsitsa beach and then another when the two of them returned to the UK. John Harris and Zoë Wilkins met in Atsitsa, too, and are now married and have a young son.

'Magically successful'

The picture of Skyros painted by numerous journalists, Carmel Thomason wrote in the *Manchester Evening News* [56], is that of 'paradise from which you return transformed'. She could not believe it before getting there as 'you don't become a journalist without being incredibly questioning about life'. Yet on her return, she praised Skyros to the skies. Everybody who comes back from Skyros does the same, novelist Maeve Binchy likewise said in *The Irish Times* [57]. Many, indeed, fall in love with it.

One of them was Sue Townsend. 'I immediately fell in love with the place as everybody does' she wrote in *The Guardian* [58]. 'I kept thinking, "I am an actor in A Midsummer Night's Dream; this is Arcadia, I want to live like this for ever".' So inspired by it, Townsend even sent Adrian Mole to Skyros for a holiday course. Connections with Atsitsa are sometimes so powerful that people even want their ashes scattered in its beautiful pine forest – Andreas Vetsch, our remarkable Atsitsa yoga facilitator who died in 2017 and whom we miss dearly, was the latest.

Skyros' reception by the media has, indeed, been overwhelming. *Elle* [59] magazine described Skyros as 'magically successful thanks to its unique alchemy of people, settings and ideals', Matthew Collins in the *BBC Travel Show* [60] portrayed it as an 'amazing place' and the *Athens News Agency* [61] extolled its human values, 'the values our society should consider all important but seldom does'. Skyros could now proudly claim, *The Guardian* [62] pointed out, that it is 'the first and still the best' alternative holiday. Or, according to *The Sunday Times* [63], 'one of the world's best holidays' offering its guests, not just the usual, but 'the finer things' [64]. 'Let your hair down, take risks, expand horizons, go on a Skyros holistic holiday,' Mariella Frostrup urged her *Independent* [65] readers.

Comments from participants, Hetty Einzig wrote in *Time Out* [66], 'run into superlatives – liberation, rejuvenation, bliss in massive doses. The memory of that fortnight', she said, 'sends ripples through our notions of real life'. 'Civilisation', Anne-Marie Conway stated similarly in *The Times Educational Supplement* [67], 'will never look quite the same'. 'It was a magical fortnight. I felt absolutely liberated', Diana Jones added in the *Woman and Home* [68]. Tony Crisp in *Yoga Today* was grateful for his Atsitsa experience that took him and others 'beyond boundaries'. Skyros, incidentally, has been described in *The Daily Telegraph* [69] as 'one of the best yoga holidays on the planet'.

Some magic at work

Similar comments appeared in features in many other publications including the Spanish daily *El Pais*, the Swedish daily *Aftonbladet* [70], the German *Suddeutsche Zeitung* [71] or Japanese journals [72]. *The Times* [73] pointed out that Skyros had turned into 'the most talked about holistic holiday destination in Europe'. 'It has become,' Tom Fordyce wrote in the same newspaper later [74], 'the sophisticated urbanite's retreat of choice.'

What won over the media, Angela Wigglesworth wrote in the *Financial Times* [75], was 'some magic at work that inspires people'. Saying the same but in different words, the *BBC Radio Four* Breakway programme [76] hailed the fact that people were 'popping up like flowers', to which Anne Karpf added in *The Journal of Alternative & Complementary Medicine* [77]: 'Almost everyone opened up. Some said it was their best holiday ever and several were on their second or even twentieth visit'. *Fitness* publisher Gail Tressider said the same in fewer words: 'Simply the best holiday I ever had – it worked on every level'.

Skyros, Jane Salvage summed up in her book *Skyros, Island of Dreams*, 'is magical, challenging, transformative, sensual, adventurous, creative, joyful, unique, revolutionary, experimental, communal, solitary – all this and more'. Simple as it may appear, it all takes skilled leadership to make it work. This is provided, amongst other things, by the teaching staff, whose quality, as Leslie Kenton stated in the *Harpers & Queen* [78] magazine, is 'very high'.

The concept of leadership in the Skyros world, of course, has a different colour. The aim is to create a community of leaders rather than followers of the enlightened one.

Beyond the corners of the ideal

But all the fun aside, Skyros has also been very tough at times. That was, for example, the day a woman, who had started seeing ghosts at night and was happy enough to share a few glasses of wine with them, was sent back to Athens for medical attention. But soon after she had got on the ferry, a very short message landed on Atsitsa's answering machine. It had been left by Johny T, a larger than life Greek-American member of staff, who was accompanying her on her return trip to Athens. The message, in three words only, informed us: 'She jumped off'. That was all. He meant off the ferry. Shocked, I tried desperately, together with Peter Webb, the Atsitsa manager, to find out what had happened, only to discover on the harbour's pavement Johny T's sense of humour, in tatters, begging for our forgiveness. 'It was only a joke', he said when he eventually answered his phone.

A similar story occurred when we were celebrating the arrival of the new millennium. One of the sixty or so guests, a woman of uncertain temper, announced as soon as she disembarked that she had come to Skyros to kill herself. The choice was to send her back to Athens, where given the effervescence of the times she was bound to welcome in the new millennium in ways she would later on, or perhaps in her afterlife, regret forever, or keep her on the island and take responsibility for her life. We kept her with us, but she needed supervision 24 hours a day, which we were happy to provide. But she had also decided to come out and, in a state of controlled hysteria, she refused help from the males of the group.

Exhausted, we asked the female guests for help, which was generously offered. But the problems still persisted one way or another. Despite being guarded, the woman often, for example, would walk out of her room into the village at 3.00 or 4.00 am and disappear in its labyrinthine streets, the island's Bermuda Triangle. The whole staff and several guests, summoned from their beds and as pale as a lemon that had just heard bad news, had no choice but

99

to start searching for her everywhere they could go. At the end, all went as well as one could hope for. She did not commit suicide, though several of us thought of doing so, and she returned home gleaming like a white stone in the rain! The letter she then sent us read: 'Thank you for the very good care you took of me.'

These stories are the property of the distant past which, when recalled, fill me with a sadness that no tablets can negotiate with. But they have all ended happily - much to the disappointment, of course, of *The Sun*, the *Daily Express* or the *News of World* . What a 'good New Age' story an unhappy ending would have provided them with!

Skyros Island

The history of Skyros island goes back to the Neolithic period (5500 – 2800 BC) and the early Bronze Age (2800 – 1900 BC). Palamari, the well-fortified village close to Atsitsa, is one of its most important prehistoric settlements (2500 - 1800 BC) with commercial links that extended as far as Syria and Palestine. Excavations carried out in the area have led to the discovery of a well-organised village with a port, roads and tall and impressive buildings.

The Mycenaean period (1650 – 1100 BC) was the time the island reached the height of its power and prosperity. Theseus, the Athenian hero who had killed the dreaded Minotaur of Crete, died there. The castle that dominates the village, probably built during the Bronze Age above the Cyclopean walls and towers on which Brooke Square now rests, was the place where Achilles was hidden by his mother to escape his fate in the war against Troy. Odysseus made sure he did not. In 475 BC, the island became part of the Athenian Empire and was colonized by its settlers until its occupation by the Romans in 192 BC. It was then taken over by the Byzantines, who rebuilt its castle. The monastery of Saint George, built on the ruins of an ancient temple by the Emperor Nikiforos Fokas in 960 AD, is still intact.

Skyros changed hands again in 1204 when the Crusaders occupied Constantinople and the island passed under the control of the Venetians. The latter, to defend themselves against marauding pirates, rebuilt its castle. In 1538, the island was conquered by the Ottomans until Greece won its independence in 1929.

Rupert Brooke, the English poet, who died in a ship anchored near Skyros island in 1915, during the First World War, is buried in a tranquil olive grove on the southern part of the island, that 'corner of a foreign field that is forever England'.

100

The island, with a population these days of about 3,000, is still off the tourist map of Greece – no mass tourism, high-rise hotels or tourist hooliganism. Fully maintaining its traditional character, it is warm and open – doors are left unlocked, young children play unattended in the streets, weddings are celebrated by the entire community, and tourists, initially viewed with curiosity, are welcome in the ancient spirit of philoxenia. If this takes the tourists back in time, the local trendy youth, enjoying the latest in fashion, the social media and the vibrant night life, takes them, on the other hand, straight to the present. Skyros, 'sunshine for the soul', as one of our visitors described it, literally lives in more than one century at once!

The links between The Skyros Centre and Atsitsa, on the one hand, and the local community, on the other, that developed over the years are based on mutual respect. Facilitators and course participants have always treated the locals with solicitude, honour their culture and enjoy the opportunities for enlarging their own horizons they offer. They happily join, in this respect, the various local celebrations including, when possible, the island's famous goat festival whose roots are traced in the Dionysian celebrations of ancient Greece and which draws visitors from all over the world. They do, on the other hand, welcome locals to various events such as music and singing evenings and also parties held at either Atsitsa or the Skyros Centre.

The locals, in turn, appreciate all the benefits that Skyros Holidays offers the island, including, of course, all those offered by the many hundreds of guests who would not have come to the island or even Greece if not for the Skyros Centre and Atsitsa. Skyros Holidays indeed makes a substantial contribution to the island's welfare.

In the Isle of Wight

In 2004, together with Christine Schulz, my partner, I moved to Shanklin, in the Isle of Wight, where we turned The Grange, a gorgeous Georgian house in the old village, into a micro-Skyros. Weekend courses in creative writing, yoga, art, personal development or music and singing immediately became available to the delight of Charlotte Hofton, the Isle of Wight *County Press* reporter. [79]

She was pleased, as she wrote in a full page story, to come across Yannis, the Grange's 'thrillingly romantic Greek owner', and Christine, 'his fragrant partner', and hear about 'their revolutionary leisure concept'. In a burst of tense eloquence, she even found my strong Greek accent 'swooningly attractive' – for better or worse, just like Henry Kissinger or Arsene Wenger,

101

I cannot replace it with something more agreeable to British ears. Hofton had visited us after she had read a two pages-long feature in *The Sunday Telegraph* [80] on a Grange course in Literotica, which one of its reporters had taken. The establishment of The Grange had started making little undulating waves in the national media.

Then, in 2007, the spirit of the new routine was interrupted when Skyros moved its HQ from London to Shanklin. The electronics revolution had made it possible. It would have even been possible in the nineties, the time I met two British architects in Tenerife who, as they said, could manage their UK business in the Canaries as easily as they did in London.

The transfer of the Skyros HQ to Shanklin was not trouble-free. Instead of the experienced Skyros admin staff, we had to rely on locals, familiar as a rule neither with the Skyros concept and its routines nor with its numerous facilitators or past participants. Still the operation turned out to be a success, but this only thanks to Christine's total commitment to the venture. She had first visited Skyros as a course participant in 1990, and then again as a workscholar for the next three years before joining the Skyros' HQ in London for a while. In love with the venture, she ensured that its new HQ in the Isle of Wight had the proper structure, the right approach, plenty of new ideas and a mellow atmosphere which contributed a lot to the smooth functioning of the whole operation.

Her total involvement gave me the chance to spend my days working on my tan. But I did not take it. Instead, I finished *The Cultural Challenge*, my trilogy, and also the autobiography of my generation that was published under the title *History, Politics and Dreams*. Soon after came my first political thriller, *The Lure of Illusions*, a story that takes place in war-torn Syria. 'I'm a successful man', I reassured myself if, of course, success is doing what you want to do as opposed to what you have to.

Yet one can never tell what the future has in store!

A distinguished staff

Skyros has been blessed with the support over the years from numerous excellent course facilitators, the best in their fields, without whom it could never be what it is. They all contributed not just their skills, but also their sprightliness and enthusiasm for the venture plus suggestions, plans and ideas, all of which helped Skyros to develop. Skyros cannot help but be grateful to them for their prodigious presence in everything that shaped it. Below is a list of as many of them as possible.

The Writing courses have attracted as facilitators established authors including Hilary Mantel, Sue Townsend, Hanif Kureishi, Margaret Drabble, Alison Lurie, Steven Berkoff, Sophie Hannah, James Kelman, Rachel Billington, Louise Doughty, Wendy Cope, Bernice Rubens, D.M. Thomas, Hugo Williams, Andrew Davies, Marina Warner, Michelle Roberts, Andrew Miller, Romesh Gunesekera, Monique Roffey, Andrew Morton, Stephen Clarke, Shelley Weiner, Susan Elderkin, Tony Hawks, Charles Pallister, Marina Lewycka, Graeme Simsion, Clare Boylan, Helena Drysdale, Lisa O'Donnell, DJ Connell, Amanda Smyth, Julia Bell, Steve Attridge, Mez Packer, Crysse Morrison, Michael Dibdin and many others.

Skyros, 'the doyenne of alternative holidays', as Gemma Bowes described it in *The Observer* [81], did also welcome other celebrities such as Hollywood actor Bob Wisdom, film directors Ken Russell and Anna Campion, filmmaker Julian Doyle, Radio DJ Mike Read, singer-songwriters Frankie Armstrong, Tom Robinson, Dean Friedman and Tom Morley, singer and actress Toyah Willcox, guitarist John Etheridge and composer and flautist Tim Wheater, actresses Polly James and Annabelle Apsion, health and beauty specialist Leslie Kenton, sculptor Glyn Williams and painter Robert Venosa, performers Arthur Smith, Logan Murray, John Cremer and Andy Ford, US environmental campaigner Kirkpatrick Sale and many others.

But it is not just the big names that Skyros can attract. It also attracts, as Janet Barcroft put it in *Here's Health* [82], 'some of the world's best teachers'. Many of them, including Silke Ziehl, Judith Hammond, Hazel Carey, Bob Shelley, Alison Goldie, Gaie Houston, Michael Eales, Malcolm Stern, Sarah Warwick, Kate Daniels, Ari Badaines, Ken Eyerman, John Harris, Susie Self, Richard Layzell, Julie McNamara, Mark Gunston and others have been coming to Skyros each year – some since 1979, Skyros' very first year.

Other fine practitioners and teachers who have run courses in Skyros just a few or numerous times since Skyros was established in the field of psychology include Judi Ledward, Julian Russell, Suzy Greaves, Alan Dale, Jan Day, Claire Schrader, Viyog Gilbert, Janie Wilson, Ernie Woolf, Helen Mundy, Ann Dunbar, Andrew Risner, Robin Shohet, Nick Price, Jurgen Wolff, Marcia Karp, Tom Kelly, Bernie Raden, Jeremiah Abrams, Natalie Rodgers, Geoff Warburton, Pat Ceccarelli, Pia Keiding-Larssen, Christina Hagelthorn, Dorothy Rowe, Jenny Biancardi, Marianne Gubler, Max Furlaud, Ake Hogberg, Dan Miller, Sue von Baeyer, Malcolm Parlett, Tom Feldberg and Anne Dickson.

The yoga teachers include Andreas Vetsch, Kym Suttle, Lisehanne Webster, Katrina Love Senn, Michael Stewart, David Moreno, Sharon Moon,

Sevanti Attwood, Martha Salonidou, David Swenson, Anastasia Stoyannides, Ulrike Harris, Tony Crisp, Gill Edwards, Derek and Radha Ireland and Stewart Mitchell.

The art teachers include Roz Wates, Cate Whittemore, Stoney Parsons, Michael Gahagan, Sarah Livingstone, Jonathan Newey, Liz De'Ath, Kevin Dibb, Peter Murphy, Ilene Sawka, Leigh Hyams, Muriel Soriano, Naomi Hunt, Madeleine Cunningham, Bobby Stuart, Peter Byrne and Jill Bennett plus photography teachers such as David Babsky and Kel Portman. The music and singing teachers include Claire Healy, Phil Haiselden, Helen Yeomans, Tom Toomey, Chloe Goodchild, Abbie Lathe, Trixie Field, Chris MacLeod, Richard Lewis, Shannon Harris, Jenni Roditi, Peter Wiegold, Anne Lister, Ossey Osmond and Ross Loraine. The dance teachers include Jo Hardy, Cathy Skora, Zoe Artemis, Kinny Gardner, Christiane Darley, Polly Benge, Claire Hayes, Katharyn Howd Machan, Amanda Stern, Maro Stoyannides, Mariko Takayasu, Merle Van den Bosch, Marcia Plevin, Marcia Leventhall, Audrey Jolly, Judy Sharpe and Bob Carlisle.

The theatre and comedy teachers include Jonathan Kay, Kate Smurthwaite, Karen Hayley, Ailon Freedman, Paul McDowell, Rachel Caine, Araxi Utidjian and Alastair MacMillan. Bodywork teachers include Alan Herdman, Virginia Evangelou, Jens Johannsen, Anthy Katsiotis, Lucy Rush, Christine Trotter, Edel Swords, Angela Davies, Judith Huggan, Rosslyn Albright, Richard Brennan, Mario-Paul Cassar, Andy Fagg and Teddy Dunn. Other facilitators include Paul Rebillot, Berny Woodward, Deborah Sanderson, John Bolwell, Hazel Carey, David Zucker, Allegra Taylor, Mandy Wheeler, Janet Marks, Mari Hall, Francis Kay, Peta Heskell, Titus Alexander, Michael Stone, Guy Claxton, Tim Le Mare, Eric Rees, Leo Rutherford, Angus Clark, Monica Harding, Nick Williams, Hong Guang Liu, John Button, Bill Palmer, Yaro Starak, Lawrence Temple, Gerry Thompson, Christine Hocking, Satish Kumar, Ian Williamson, Gunila Ambjörnsson, Ake Hogberg, Sharon Clough, Marcia Leventhal and Jacques Salzer. Also windsurfing teachers John Wigham and Simon Wilson.

Special mention should also be made of all the Skyros island 'permanent' staff, which has kept Skyros going through thick and thin. This includes the administrative staff – among others, Pam Chaplin, Julian Colborn, Peter Webb and Michael Eales, to name just a few – and also chefs, gardeners, and work scholars. They have all been part of the Skyros community and contributed, like the facilitators, massively to turn Skyros into a 'world-famous' holiday [83]. We have been very privileged to have them.

104

References

1. Clive Leighton, The Birmingham Post, 17 March 2007

2. Anne Roper, Sunday Independent (Ireland), 10 January 1999

3. Lynn Wallis, Evening Standard, 23 May 2002

4. https://www.skyros.com/holiday-locations/greece-atsitsa-bay/oekos/

5. Wendy Roberts, Derby Telegraph, 1 December 2011

6. https://www.skyros.com/holiday-locations/greece-atsitsa-bay/co-listening/

7. Judith Linder, The Observer, 25 August 2002
   https://www.theguardian.com/travel/2002/aug/25/travellingsolo.observerescapesection

8. Deirdre Mullins, Independent.i.e, 11 February 2018
   https://www.independent.ie/life/travel/europe/solo-in-skyros-how-to-start-yournovel-on-a-sun-holiday-34916525.html

9. Elle, June 2005

10. The Guardian, 7 June 2008
    https://www.theguardian.com/travel/2008/jun/07/culturaltrips.fivebest

11. Rachael Oakes-Ash, The Age, Melbourne, 8 September 2014
    http://www.executivestyle.com.au/the-worlds-best-writers-retreats-10d2dw

12. Independent, 25 September 2004
    http://www.independent.co.uk/arts-entertainment/books/features/the-isles-ofinspiration-34331.html

13. Jane Salvage, Skyros, the Island of Dreams

14. Kate Birch, Aquarius Magazine, UAE, 1 March 2012

15. Lizzie Enfield, Sunday Times, 6 July 2008
    https://www.thetimes.co.uk/article/my-hols-jimmy-carr-88lfmdnsfkm

16. Red magazine, August 2008

17. The Daily Telegraph. 1 July 2016,
    http://www.telegraph.co.uk/travel/destinations/europe/greece/articles/your-favourite-greek-islands/

18. Judith Linder, The Observer, 25 August 2002

19. Joan Scales, Irish Times, 25 February 2012

20. Trudi Orchard, Elle, September 2005

21. Leah Hellen, Top Sante. June 2003 18. Sharon Garfinkel, Jewish Chronicle, 7 March 2007
    See also Sharron Livingston, The Jewish Chronicle, 1 January 2016
    https://www.thejc.com/lifestyle/travel/holidays/my-kind-of-retreat - 1.56693

22. Kate Rew, The Observer, 19 June 2005
    https://www.theguardian.com/travel/2005/jun/19/greece.observerescapesection

23. 10. Cathy Wilson, Huffington Post, 29 June 2015 http://www.huffingtonpost.co.uk/cathy-winston/solo-travel_b_7662662.html

24. Kate Edgley, The Age. Melbourne, 25 February 2012

25. Lesley Garner, The Sunday Telegraph, 2 January 1993

26. Kate Weinberg, Evening Standard, 25 April 2007

27. Janet Watts, The Observer, 5 November 1995

28. Hugo Williams, The Times Literary Supplement, 29 October 1993

29. The Daily Telegraph, 5 July 2008

30. Barbara Gunnell, The Observer, 23 July 1989

31. Angela Neustatter, The Times, 16 April 1994

32. Deb Hunt, Sunday Telegraph, Sydney, March 2004

33. Rebecca Taylor, Time Out, 5 May 2004

34. Jackie Pilkington, The Daily Telegraph, 1 July 2016 http://www.telegraph.co.uk/travel/destinations/europe/greece/articles/your-favourite-greek-islands/

35. Melissa de Villiers, Red magazine, January 1999

36. Ailbhe Brilley, The Irish Times, 6 March 2010 https://www.irishtimes.com/life-and-style/travel/bending-and-bonding-on-a-greekbeach-1.634057

37. Bruno Latzelsperger, The Globe and Mail (Canada), 28 March 2016 https://www.theglobeandmail.com/life/travel/activities-and-interests/five-writingretreats-around-the-globe-to-kick-start-your-creativejuices/article29402696/

38. Roisin Ingle, The Irish Times, 7 June 2008 https://www.irishtimes.com/life-and-style/travel/greece-lightning-1.1217491

39. Tracey Jennings, Health and Fitness magazine, September 2004

40. ITV's First Tuesday, 7 September 1993

41. Mary Comber, Health & Fitness, September 2004

42. Sharron Livingston, The Travel Magazine, 28 September 2015 http://www.thetravelmagazine.net/skyros-community-based-holistic-retreat.html

43. Damian Barr, The Times, 24 April 2004 https://www.thetimes.co.uk/article/hopes-but-no-glory-jbgtgd9zm2g

44. The Irish Times, 22 September 2007 https://www.irishtimes.com/life-and-style/shanti-town-1.964765

45. Michèle Roberts, The New Statesman, 22 August 2005 https://www.newstatesman.com/node/198506

46. Paul Mansfield, The Sunday Telegraph, 18 February 1996

47. Moyra Bremner, The Guardian, 20 October 2001

48. Claire Droney, Irish Examiner, 2 January 2016
https://www.irishexaminer.com/lifestyle/travel/bigread/a-letter-from-paradise-onthe-greek-island-ofskyros-373889.html

49. Crysse Morrison, The Times, 31 December 2011

50. Andrea Anastasiou, 16 October 2015
http://www.scribblesnaptravel.com/how-a-skyros-writing-retreat-changed-my-life-and-why-you-should-also-consider-a-retreat-holiday/

51. John Hargreaves, Here's Health, May 1994

52. Anne Roper, Sunday Independent, 10 January 1999

53. Peta Heskell, The Guardian, 5 December 2003
https://www.theguardian.com/travel/2003/dec/05/bestplacefor

54. Andrea Smith, Independent.ie, 26 December 2010
https://www.independent.ie/lifestyle/suzanne-and-albie-start-a-new-chapter-in-life-of-love-26609091.html

55. Cosmopolitan, August 1998

56. Carmel Thomason, Manchester Evening News, 18 April 2010

57. Ailbhe Brilley, The Irish Times, 6 March 2010
https://www.irishtimes.com/life-and-style/travel/bending-and-bonding-on-a-greekbeach-1.634057

58. Sue Townsend, The Guardian, 26 September 1998

59. Elissa Van Poznak, Elle magazine, September 2005

60. BBC Travel Show, 22 June 1989 and then again on 21 September 1991 and on 5 August 1993

61. Athens News Agency, 10 November 1987

62. The Guardian online, 20 March 2008

63. Stephen Bleach, The Sunday Times, 6 January 2008
https://www.thetimes.co.uk/article/100-summer-holidays-for-08-3xtdxw686x7

64. Stephen Bleach, The Sunday Times, 10 January 2010

65. Mariella Frostrup, Independent, 2001

66. Hetty Einzig, Time Out, 20 August 1986

67. Anne Marie Conway, Times Educational supplement, 22 January 1988

68. Diana Jones, Woman and Home, September 2003

69. Caroline Sylger-Jones, The Daily Telegraph, 19 June 2017
http://www.telegraph.co.uk/travel/spas/best-yoga-holidays-in-the-world/

70. Margareta Wasterstram, Aftonbladet, 26 February 1989

71. Kaevan Gazdar, Süddeutsche Zeitung, 16 March 1993

72. Asahi Weekly, Japan – 18 September 2016

73. The Times Online, 19 June 2007

74. Tom Fordyce, The Times, 8 March 2010

75. Angela Wigglesworth, Financial Times, 9 May 1998

76. BBC Radio 4, Breakway, 21 September 1991

77. Anne Karpf, Journal of Alternative and Complementary Medicine, July 1989

78. Leslie Kenton, Harpers & Queen

79. Charlotte Hofton, the Isle of Wight County Press http://www.iwcp.co.uk/news/finding-true-happiness-beyond-barnsley-9421.aspx

80. Jeremy Clarke, The Sunday Telegraph, 29 May 2005

81. Gemma Bowes, The Observer, 20 March 2005 https://www.theguardian.com/

82. Janet Barcroft, Here's Health, May 1994

83. Victoria Lambert, The Daily Telegraph, 14 May 2018 and also National Post (Canada), 18 May 2018

5. Dreamers & Doers: An Inspirational Team

Flying high on the wings of your vision

Skyros, 'the first and still the best' alternative holiday, has turned into a flag-bearer for holistic living.

In this it was helped by both its vision and also the commitment to it and the professionalism of its facilitators, administrators and other members of its staff.

Space does not permit the presentation of all the people who have helped to turn the dream into reality. Featured in the next few pages are therefore only those who have been working with Skyros for years and years – some as many as thirty or more! – and are an indispensable part of Skyros' history.

We are hugely thankful to them and also all the others for their magnificent contribution to a venture that offered so much to the thousands of participants who joined it over the years.

The number next to each name under a photo marks the year the facilitators joined the Skyros venture – the time Skyros became part of their life. A few of them have now passed away, but they live on in our hearts.

Christine Schulz, Skyros' Managing Director, joined Skyros as a participant in 1990, a workscholar from 1991 to 1993, and in 2004 moved to the Isle of Wight to set up The Grange, later to become Skyros HQ.

Bodywork Practitioner, Silke Ziehl, first joined Skyros in 1979 and has since been absolutely vital to Skyros up in terms of her essential advice, caring support, practical help and unfailing commitment to Skyros and its aims.

Ari Badaines (1981)   Tom Kelly (1982)   Tom Feldberg (1982)

David Zucker (1983)   Gaie Houston (1983)   Richard Layzell (1984)

Julie McNamara (1984)   Jenni Roditi (1985)   Malcolm Stern (1986)

112

Judy Hammond (1986)   Hazel Carey (1986)   Radha Ireland (1987)

Derek Ireland (1987)   Frankie Armstrong (1987)   Lisehanne Webster (1988)

Judi Ledward (1989)   Ken Eyerman (1989)   Bob Shelley (1990)

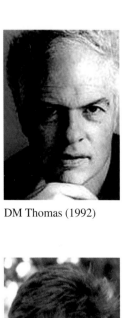

DM Thomas (1992)   Michael Eales (1992)   Nell Dunn (1992)

Hugo Williams (1993)   Allegra Taylor (1993)   Marcia Karp (1994)

Sue Townsend (1994)   A. Stoyannides (1995)   Mark Gunston (1996)

114

Alison Goldie (1997)　　John Wigham (1997)　　Richard Lewis (1997)

Kel Portman (1998)　　Steve Attridge (1998)　　Virginia Evangelou (1999)

Viyog Gilbert (1999)　　Roz Wates (1999)　　Tom Robinson (1999)

Kate Daniels (2000)   Susie Self (2000)   Margaret Drabble (2000)

Carthy Skora (2000)   Julian Doyle (2001)   Sevanti (2001)

Clare Boylan (2001)   Berny Woodward (2001)   Michael Stewart (2001)

116

Sophie Hannah (2001)   Stoney Parsons (2002)   Sarah Warwick (2002)

Andrew Risner (2002)   Crysse Morrison (2003)   Andreas Vetsch (2003)

Julia Bell (2006)   Monique Roffey (2008)   David Babsky (2008)

117

Arthur Smith (2008)   Michael Gahagan (2009)   Amanda Smyth (2010)

Theresa Sundt (2010)   Logan Murray (2011)   Marina Sossi (2011)

Shelley Weiner (2011)   Tom Morley (2012)   Mez Packer (2012)

118

And a few of
the managerial
staff plus chefs
and others

Ailon Freedman (2013)   Leigh Russell (2013)

Andy Mullett   Niko Sikkes   Pamela Chaplin

Julian Colborn   Peter Webb   Jane Reed

119

John Harris   Zoë Harris   Mark Shaw

Wallee McDonnell   Rhona Donaldson   George Evgenicos

Vasso Triantafyllou   Manolis Xanthoulis   Taki Koutsoupis

120

6. The Joy of Living

A drink in the village: one portion of wine and two of water

Enjoying the view from Rupert Brooke Square

Picking jasmine from a street close to the market

Sunbathe, play and enjoy the blessings of leisure on Skyros beach

125

New and old songs engulf the village square with their melodies

In the village's Calypso bar. You can sit anywhere. No cars

126

The village has not experienced tourism's personality transplant

Honey balls for everyone during a wedding

127

Sue Townsend in town, window shopping, and traditional Skyrian dance

The financial crisis bites hard but spirits are high

128

Streets with friendly faces and tourists by the statue of Rupert Brooke

Members of The Skyros Centre ready to join the carnival

A song the colour of the sea and Atsitsa's forest

The heart-stoppingly beautiful Atsitsa Bay from the hill above

131

Atsitsa's stunning surroundings

Huts in the Atsitsa garden under pine and fruit trees

132

The heart of Atsitsa

In the company of flowers

Apricots in Atsitsa's fruit garden

They wouldn't let Atsitsa's almonds go to waste

134

Vivid pine green and sparkling Aegean blue

Urns in Atsitsa from the time of Alexander the Great, found in the sea nearby

Exploring the merits of a Mediterranean diet and a well-balanced life

Lunchtime in Atsitsa

136

Enjoying meals together out in the open

Wow! What a treat!

137

From the beach 4/08   Jacques ©

A picture is a poem without words

138

Poet Hugo Williams at the Writers' Lab at The Skyros Centre

Dina Glouberman running her 'Life Choices, Life Changes' course

140

Monique Roffey inspiring a group of Writers' Lab participants

Author Shelley Weiner leading a writing session beneath the grapevines

141

Margaret Drabble running her course at The Skyros Centre

Making useful notes before writing the next chapter of her book

142

Surrendering to the aura of mystery below the surface of the sea

Yoga held in Atsitsa's gardens

143

Moved by the spirit of the sun and the scent of the sea

Atsitsa brings out the inner artist ·

144

The fabulous trapeze is not everybody's choice of pleasure

Monique's group taking a break during a walk in the island's forest

145

Raqs Sharqi on the left. Abseiling on the right

Peter Webb celebrates his half-Marathon win, and Theresa Sundt with her rainbow artwork

146

Working on her novel before a day out on Atsitsa's sailing boat

Windsurfing for beginners – and the advanced, too

Singer-songwriter Frankie Armstrong (far right) leading her group

What spring does with the cherry trees. Flowering in the Magic Circle

148

Glynn Williams, the sculptor, and Dean Friedman, the singer-songwriter

Painting on the beach and sharing their dreams with the sea

149

A wonderful piece of stained glass by Stoney Parson's group

An early evening viewing of everyone's artwork

Mark Gunston cruising in the Aegean just before he got a speeding ticket

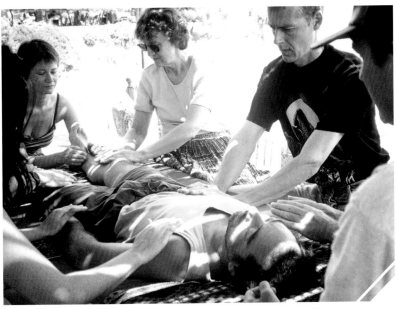

Learning the art of massage between drinks of fresh peach juice

151

A painting inspired by the beauty of Atsitsa

Heaven: beautiful environment, creative work

152

The joy of singing with Sarah Warwick

Camaraderie and sharing in Atsitsa's Magic Circle

153

In tune with nature's rhythms

154

III. Adventure, Creativity, Joy

Where dreams sometimes come true and new dreams are born

Ailon Freedman and Andreas Vetsch trying to unlock what's not locked

Eyes twinkling with good humour. Lauren & Melissa

David Zucker is flirting again with a local

157

Amanda Simpson sings in the village square. Richard Lewis on the saxophone

Marina Sossi, the yoga teacher, announces the arrival of lunch

158

Hear! Hear! Hear! We had a fantastic fortnight at The Skyros Centre

A song on Atsitsa's balcony overlooking the bay

159

They don't seem to miss their social media connections

Taken like the trees and rocks by the sound of the music

Sarah Helena and Carly Marie on Skyros village beach

Individuals but together rather than apart

Beyond all the trivial events of the day

Maybe not mad – just crazy

Odile Petrie, Atsitsa's French chef, joins the party in 1985

Richard Layzell elevating common pretensions to a higher level

The evening's embodiment of the absurd. Cupids and satyrs are singing

When the spirits of the night are on the loose

A night of The Full Moon

All musical talents find a place in Atsitsa's band

The kitchen staff's naughty sense of humour. But their food is delicious

166

Rehearsing their piece before presenting it in the Atsitsa cabaret

Alison Goldie and John Wigham investigate a 'murder' in Atsitsa

167

Comedian Arthur Smith shares a joke at the Skyros Centre

Actor and writer Stephen Berkoff addresses the Atsitsa crowd

168

Ossey Osmond of the Barron Knights and Tom Robinson get ready for action

So much to chat about over lunch

169

Atsitsa's alco-holistic bar

People loved John Wigham's French café in Atsitsa

Yannis in 1992. Ready for action in the clowning workshop

Not as lonely as our belly buttons. Atsitsa participants enjoying a night out

As cheerful as swallows in the Spring

Words can sometimes be drummed

Workscholars are never shy to join the fun

Some know everything about life except how to enjoy it. Not this group

173

Caroline in the midst of flowers and friends

A riotous evening dancing in Atsitsa's bar

174

Another way of making a statement

Daring to open wide their wings and take flight to new skies

175

Claire Healy enthusing the crowd with a breathless, inarticulate excitement

Crazy not to enjoy this madness. A weird reenactment of a Euripides play

176

Three cheers to this lovely place

We played, we sang, we drank water fresh from the spring of life

Atsitsa fun. A moment neither of them has forgotten

Shoulders shaken by laughter. Kate Daniels (left) and friend

A band brought together by the songs they love

She can't help herself. It's irresistible

179

Perhaps on their way to the local supermarket?

Another way to keep in touch with each other

180

Happy like the stream that laughs its way down the hill

Taki and the group will take care of your birthday

Tom Morley leads the radiant crowd

A celebration of life as Atsitsa celebrates this lady's birthday

Time for this and time for that. Time for romance, too

Individuality and togetherness go hand in hand

Evenings in Atsitsa are full of fun

Flower power as in the old days many still remember

184

They don't need to be entertained. They can entertain themselves

Irresistible honey balls for dessert: essential for a balanced life

A drink before dinner and the evening's music show

Winding their way back to Atsitsa through the pine forest

186

Dina addressing the Atsitsa community meeting

Dancing on midnight's floor to the frenzied drums

187

Romantic attachments are as good as gold but not as rare

Veggie chopping in the best of company

A fine balancing act! Even Andrew seems surprised

An atmospheric evening event

Who's teasing Pop? Sue in tune with the rhythm of sunset

Life can be very colourful but growth can take unexpected forms

Spiritually uplifting moments

Enjoying the prime blessings of leisure

Always time for a song

Much better here than on London's Northern Line

This Canadian couple were married in Atsitsa. Hundreds joined the party

Skyros is the moment but it is also the future

Life as it is lived at home is no longer viewed as destiny

194

Time for a hundred visions and revisions

In the loving arms of Atsitsa's turquoise sea

196

7. Skyros, Island of Dreams

By Jane Salvage

Jane Salvage is well known in the UK and worldwide for her leadership in nursing and healthcare development, and for her widely read publications. She has held senior posts with the Prime Minister's Commission on the Future of Nursing and Midwifery in England, the Willis Commission on Nursing Education, the World Health Organization (WHO), the Nursing Times magazine, the King's Fund and elsewhere. She has been visiting Skyros island since 1991 as tourist, journalist, participant and course teacher.

This is an extract from her book *Skyros, Island of Dreams*

New visions for a new world

Both Skyros founders, in their contrasting but complementary ways, believe Skyros can help us model a different way of being. Perhaps it can even help shape a new global politics. Dina Glouberman talks of it as a micro-world, and of her work as helping people create new worlds. She describes how her research for The Joy of Burnout uncovered a characteristic pattern that may or may not end in burnout, depending on how the person responds to a crucial choice point.

'As I believe that any pattern worth its salt must be true on more than the personal level, I have begun to observe that the world situation right now is displaying elements of the same burnout pattern. This is important, because once we understand a pattern, we are able to work with it far more clearly and effectively,' she says. 'When something changes, and our heart goes out of the old situation, it is time to stop, listen to the soul whisperings, and wait until we find a way forward. We don't know what to do but we need to find out.'

This is certainly how it was after September 11, 2001, she says. 'We knew that terrorism was not a battle we could fight with the old weapons, or with our old knowhow, and we needed to find a new way. We also knew that without understanding the reason behind the terrorism, we could never hope to stop it. But we headed for burnout, crashing ahead using all our old methods, trying harder and harder and accomplishing less and less.'

She sees another level of response emerging to that choice point which takes the form of world opinion: 'the sound of those listening to the world soul's whisperings, determined to burn through and not burn out. The whisperings are getting louder. There is a groundswell of something new which is asking for peace and not war, food and not weapons, love and not hate and fear. But it is also saying: How do we stop terrible dictators? And how do we deal with terrorism when we know there are so many dispossessed angry people around the world who feel this is the only way to get a hearing? How do we respond to our leaders when they are probably not listening and certainly not hearing?'

As is typical at this burnout choice point, we don't know what to do, so we have to stop and listen and open up to a bigger picture of how we conduct our politics as well as our lives. 'The path of radical healing is the same on this level as on the individual level. Among other things, it includes the decision to commit ourselves to put truth first, to take care of the spiritual wellbeing of the goose rather than the material success of the golden eggs, and to reach out to our soul community – those who operate from similar values, though they may not have the same opinions or thoughts or voting pattern, and will care for us as we truly are,' she says.

The central message from Yannis Andricopoulos is in some ways similar, although expressed very differently. His sense of hopelessness and dissatisfaction with contemporary party politics was a driving force for his early commitment to Skyros; his centre at The Grange celebrates 'beauty and subversion'; and his trilogy of books explores in depth 'the madness of our civilization and the individual's search for his or her truth'. The Future of the Past, the third part of the trilogy, challenges us all to transform society 'from the culture of profit to the culture of joy'. In its epilogue, Yannis talks of the dream of a better world as a vital feature of our unconscious landscape – 'a dream is another form of reality which challenges, surpasses and overrides the reality of the senses', he says. This may not take us that far, but maintaining the tension between reality and ideal relativises the present and de-legitimises its claims. It challenges the status quo and its structure of feelings.

The dream thus stands up against the passive surrender of the individual to the madness of a disequilibrated world, he writes. 'It enables us to confront it by remaking it in the image of our desires. The presence of the dream is the assertion of the positive over the negative, the individual's expression of solidarity with humankind. It is a vote of self-confidence which re-energises and sustains our belief in ourselves and has the power to inspire and motivate. It holds us together in the pursuit of the common good.' Utopia, in other words, is an educator.

Recognising that dreams of Utopia have been out of fashion for a generation, Yannis argues that the utopian impulse is nevertheless part of our nature. 'We cannot do without a vision of the future in which our desires, fantasies, cravings and wishes for a better world, sometimes unconscious, are met, as we cannot live without hope', he says. This unfolding of new and enthralling possibilities, as many as the imagination can produce, is what gives life its substance and direction. So he calls for a renewal of utopian thinking – not just as an airy-fairy fantasy, but through engagement for the purpose of society's critical faculties and the development of its members' creative thinking. This – the arena, he says, where 'the attainable and the unattainable meet and look curiously at one another' – will help us in our continuing struggle against a society that is normless, self-centred, and driven by greed, special interests, and an unabashed quest for power.

To be utopian means to make a critical assessment of the present as seen from a distance, 'a different perspective which helps us to rethink life, explore alternatives and inform our choices.' Although Yannis does not mention Skyros, it is impossible to read his words without thinking of it. By making real their dream of Skyros, he and Dina have created just such an arena – where countless people over the years have rediscovered their utopian impulses and re-energised their dreams, in a kind of Utopia in the present. Its founders' exciting ways of articulating the interconnection between the personal and political are perhaps the messages the world most needs to hear from Skyros, and to learn at Skyros. Crucially and unusually, right from the beginning, Skyros has woven together the political and personal growth strands of the 'alternative' world, symbolically in its practice and in the outlook and influence of its founders. These strands are still, as then, generally polarized and in conflict, seen falsely as a dichotomy; but progress will be difficult unless we understand that it is not a question of either/or, but of both/and.

Dina believes it is helpful to 'give up hope and keep the faith', as she counsels burntout people to do. 'This means we have to give up the specific and rather desperate hope, which is in fact built on top of deep hopelessness, that change will come about in the manner and at the speed that we want it to and expect it to. Yet we must keep the faith that the voice of the world soul will eventually win out, and that we will find the way to make this happen.'

At Skyros, many of us experience how it could be possible for the voice of the world soul to win out – often for the first time in a very long while. We have a great holiday, while catching sight of the apparently unattainable and rekindling our hopes and dreams.

'Travelling in the direction of our hopes, towards the ocean of the soul's goals, we need to be prepared to sail outside our culture's perimeters, round the curves of time, into the sparkling marvels of the intimidating unknown, depending on our instinctual courage and on our own sense of direction,' Yannis concludes.

Wherever the ship of life takes us, in the uncharted waters of the future, we have briefly weighed anchor at an island of dreams: Skyros, the island where dreams sometimes come true and other new dreams are born.

Atsitsa's pelican who learned to trust the humans

Beautiful without noise, great without pretension

201

Atsitsa's sealife habitat adorned with mosaics

202

8. The Grange by the Sea

Skyros HQ, The Grange by the Sea in Shanklin's Old Village, Isle of Wight

The Grange by the Sea

Isle of Wight

The Grange by the Sea, is the winter home of Skyros as well as its head office. Its gorgeous, early nineteenth century Georgian country house is in the heart of Shanklin's Old Village, known as the 'jewel' of the Island. Nestled in greenery, it is very secluded. Yet it's only moments from the long sandy beach, thatched cottages, pubs and cosy tearooms. The local train station is just a few minutes away.

Its original features such as the ornate, carved fireplace in the lounge are complemented by a collection of paintings and sculptures ranging in style from bold and striking to classically elegant. With plenty of character and warmth, it combines historic charm with modern facilities in the provision of comfortable 4-star guest accommodation. Its 15 guest bedrooms are decorated in natural tones mirroring the surrounding environment and adorned with bold and colourful art. They are furnished to a high standard and most enjoy views of the sea or downs. Power showers and complimentary luxury toiletries ensure a good start to each day. As does the sumptuous breakfast.

The Grange weekend courses range from creative writing, comedy, music and singing to art, life coaching, photography and yoga. They are run by established Skyros facilitators, including well-known authors and leading life coaches. Special celebratory sessions are held over Christmas and New Year. Participants who join them have the chance to try something new, meet interesting people and possibly return home with new talents they never knew they possessed!

The Grange also provides B&B accommodation. It is listed in the AA's Best British B&B Guide and is repeatedly awarded TripAdvisor's Certificate of Excellence.

Blessed by Britain's best weather and rich in visible history – Roman villas, medieval castles and historic houses – the Isle of Wight possesses an extraordinary grace. Over half of it is preserved as an area of Outstanding Natural Beauty with lush green pastures, pristine streams and animal and bird sanctuaries. Long, sandy beaches offer a great variety of watersports, and five hundred miles of footpaths make the island a walker's paradise. For cyclists, there are a myriad of designated routes, bridleways and spectacular coastal tracks. Festivals and events jostle for position in the island's calendar – from rock and jazz concerts to extreme sports, cycling, and beach soccer events. All these, combined with the world famous sailing regatta at Cowes, have turned the island into what The Observer called 'the new cool'.

The peaceful and inspirational location of The Grange makes it the perfect venue for workshops, seminars, training events and team building activities. In its premises, organisations can develop and train their staff, help their team to work more effectively together or empower individuals to work out their future. But The Grange is also perfect for a relaxed get-together whatever the occasion – a birthday, anniversary or reunion. Its fifteen bedrooms can accommodate up to 28 guests. Aside from its picturesque grounds, other facilities include the lounge–meeting room, dining room, a licensed bar with an outdoors decking area, and a sauna, mini-gym & treatment room.

Press Reports

Charlotte Hofton, *The Isle of Wight County Press*, 10 June 2005

'I would love to enrol for anything at The Grange, where you are provided with interesting tutorials, lots of free time in which to relax, social events and group activities. Who wants to be any sort of Tuscany, anyway? Shanklin has become the new Elysium.'

Jeremy Clarke, *The Sunday Telegraph*, 29 May 2005

(Jeremy took the erotic writing course with Mitzi Szereto, which he loved.) 'Eat at the elegant dining room. Happy to watch Liverpool v AC Milan on the wide-screen television in the course during which 'neither Yannis nor I mention sex once. It is heaven'.

Sally Shalam, *Sunday Express,* 7 August 2005

(Sally took the flirting and dating bank holiday course with Alison Goldie.) What's great about a stay at The Grange is that you can really relax. It has comfy beds, crisp bed linen, en-suite power showers and, during our convivial meals, no shortage of decent wine. It's been such a fantastic weekend and I haven't laughed so much in ages.'

Top Santé, June 2006

'When you're not learning how to think positively, you can enjoy the gorgeous countryside and dine on grilled fish. You'll return home with a plan on how to achieve your goals and a whole new 'can-do' attitude.'

Spirit and Destiny, May 2006

'The Grange is the perfect place to escape the hectic pace of modern life.'

Jill Stanley-Grainger, *Healthy,* March 2007

(Jill took a Health and Wellbeing course.) 'I felt brighter and more positive than I had in months.'

Caroline Sylger Jones, *The Guardian Online,* December 2009

'The Grange by the Sea, Isle of Wight, is a stylish wellbeing retreat that won't break the bank.'

The Times, 13 August 2011

'The Grange by the Sea has a wonderful boho feel and is set in acres of rambling gardens.'

Lauris Morgan-Griffiths, *Coast Magazine,* November 2011

(Lauris took Amanda Smyth's writing course.) 'Amanda has certainly inspired the group'.

The Mirror - December 2014

'Sign up for a crash course in dating at The Grange on the Isle of Wight. Life coach Alison Goldie will cover subjects such as how you sabotage yourself and how to make the best of your assets on a fun and informative course.'

The Telegraph - 5 September 2016

'Courses are great for solo travellers or friends looking for a weekend break with a difference.'

Charlotte Bush, *Arthritis Digest* - Issue 2 2017

The Grange, this gorgeous secluded Georgian country house is nestled in greenery and offers a fantastic programme of writing courses with the help of award-winning authors.'

Lucy Thackray, *Sunday Times Travel* - January 2018

(Lucy took DJ Connell's writing course). 'I came away inspired, fired up about my premise, and armed with Diane's tricks to get the creative juices flowing.'

A Grange visitor, the red squirrel prevalent in the Isle of Wight

The Grange garden is full of colour

210

211

The lounge where courses are often held

The dining room at breakfast

The hallway in which Andrew Risner and Alison Goldie are sharing a joke

The Grange honesty bar, a place to relax

213

Plenty of paintings everywhere

One of The Grange's fifteen bedrooms

214

And hundreds of books

The dining area

A weekend writing course with Sam North

A course in breadmaking with Alison

Exchanging presents during a Christmas celebration

Jo Wood adding in the choreography with her rock choir

217

A salsa course with John Harris

Dinner with a group of academics who hired the Grange for the weekend

A course in painting and another in photography with Julian Doyle (right)

They sing and they love it

219

Yoga on the decking during a very bright morning with Andreas Vetsch

Course work in the garden

Time to explore and enjoy the beautiful landscape

Enjoying a special event and the June weather

Shanklin's old village takes visitors back in time by a few centuries

Forms of local transport – cycling on the island is a pleasure

222

Shanklin's long sandy beach is only minutes from The Grange

The annual round the island yacht race and Shanklin's carnival procession

My experience in Atsitsa in the summer of 2008

Happy 40th Anniversary

This text was emailed to the Skyros office in January 2018. Una describes her piece as 'a little Irish girl's experience of Skyros, written during my time in this amazing place'.

I step from the bus, with my chosen goals, agendas, preconceived notions. I place my heavy backpack onto the warm ground. I look around take a deep breath pause and think "ah this is where it all happens?"

I am not alone, many people gather to this same place. There is quiet chaos a nervous energy as one by one we are all allocated our private places.....

BE BRAVE

So many faces, So many voices, So many strangers. Do I get back on the bus, take my backpack and run? What have I done, Why am I here? Seemed so easy when I booked, now I'm not so sure.... Quietly I say "Be Brave"

First three days exhaust me, Talking, smiling, doing, waking, sleeping, eating - Still too many faces, too many voices So many Strangers.

224

My emotions engulf me,
I'm angry, I'm tired, I'm lonely, I'm nervous, I'm sad,
I'm judging, I'm giving, I'm taking more -

Still too many faces, too many voices, So many Strangers.

I don't want to be here, these people they are these emotions,
At breakfast, at lunch, at dinner and anytime in between,
This place so beautiful, so open, so why feel so trapped?
I pause again saying quietly "Be Brave"

As time passes the hot sun softens my body,
slows my walk, settles my thoughts.
And so it is with others
We breathe softer together, talk together, listen together,
Not So many faces, not So many voices,
not So many Strangers.

Emotions engulf me again
I'm laughing, I'm singing, I'm crying, I'm dancing,
I'm praying, I'm giving, I'm receiving, I'm hugging,
I'm sitting, I'm breathing, I'm being!

I want to be here, these people are these emotions at breakfast,
at lunch, at dinner and anytime in between
Thank God for I am blessed

As I leave, you have given me the greatest gift of all ....
MYSELF!'

My wish for you is, to just pause, BE BRAVE,
step closer, look deeper and see that there are beautiful faces,
wise voices and absolutely No Strangers!

Una McKane, Atsitsa 2008

Books by Dina Glouberman

Life Choices, Life Changes, Unwin Hyman, 1989
The Joy of Burnout, Hodder and Stoughton, 2002
You are what you Imagine, Watkins Books, 2014
Into the Woods and Out Again, Sphinx, 2018
www.dinaglouberman.com

Books by Yannis Andricopoulos

The Lure of Illusions, Arena Books, 2017
History, Politics and Dreams, Grosvenor House Pbl, 2015
The Cultural Challenge (A Trilogy), Imprint Academic, 2008
In Bed with Madness
The Greek Inheritance
The Future of the Past
Η Δημοκρατια του Μεσοπολεμου, Αθηνα, 1987
Who Were the Fascists, Universitetsforlaget, 1980
Το Ευρωπαικο Αδιεξοδο, Αθηνα, 1978
Οι Ριζες του Ελληνικου Φασισμου, Αθηνα, 1977
1944, Κρισιμη Χρονια, Αθηνα, 1974
www.yannisandricopoulos.com

226